Praise for *Now That I Think About It*

"*Now That I Think About It* offers an excellent framework for building the most important habit of mind teachers can develop in their students: reflectivity. As artificial intelligence becomes ever more pervasive in and beyond our classrooms, reflection won't just be helpful—it's going to be absolutely necessary for students to learn and succeed. The authors equip us with practical suggestions to prepare students to be critical thinkers and learners."

—**Eric C. MacDonald,** head of middle school, Benchmark School, Media, Pennsylvania

"*Now That I Think About It* is a compelling professional book that treats reflection not as an add-on but as the driving force of deep learning. Grounded in research yet full of lived classroom stories and ready-to-use protocols, it shows exactly how to make students' thinking visible and help them become more strategic, metacognitive learners across content areas. This is a practical, deeply student-centered guide for any educator who wants learning to stick!"

—**Katia Ciampa**, associate professor of literacy education, Widener University

"An invaluable resource for educators across grade levels and subject areas! The three intentional strategies for reflection—looking at, looking in, and looking out—are essential for students and teachers to master. The specific protocols and appendixes can be used immediately. I look forward to using this resource with my preservice teachers this semester!"

—**Pauline Schmidt, PhD,** professor of English education, West Chester University, and director of the West Chester Writing Project

"*Now That I Think About It* takes readers on a compelling journey into reflection, explaining its connections to inquiry, critical thinking, creating new understandings, and moving learning from short- to long-term memory. Each chapter includes authentic classroom snapshots, literacy-focused stories, ideas for helping multilingual students, and practical strategies teachers can use immediately. Bravas to the authors for showing us how to create a community of thinkers and problem solvers and for writing a book that's a terrific investment for novice, experienced, and preservice teachers, as well as coaches and teacher trainers."

—**Laura Robb,** author of *Teaching Reading in Middle School* and *Teaching in Uncertain Times*

"Reflection is a critical step in the learning process, yet it is often overlooked or an afterthought. *Now That I Think About It* is an incredibly insightful work that can serve as a guide for any practicing teacher, teacher leader, or school leader. The authors make the case for reflection as a vital imperative and then masterfully present various strategies and approaches for integrating reflection into academic practice in a way that is natural and possible—not out of reach."

—**Daniel W. Hartman, EdD,** superintendent,
Conestoga Valley School District

"This book is an invaluable resource, both for in-service sessions with teachers and for undergraduate and graduate coursework. The authors offer a compelling road map for developing reflective learners while also illuminating how educators can deepen their own reflective practice. Many books provide scaffolds and protocols for reflection, but this one goes further, explaining *how* and *why* these approaches work in a way that is clear, unique, and accessible. This is the book I wish I had during my years as a school district administrator and later as a university professor."

—**Virginia B. Modla, PhD,** retired associate professor

"A powerful blend of metaphor, brain research, and examples frame this deep dive into promoting metastrategic thinking. Clear steps, paired with authentic student and practitioner voices, deliver protocols that foster student agency, make learners feel valued, and encourage active, confident thinking. This text is a much-needed balm for hurried and often scattered thinking in our digital world."

—**Nanci Werner-Burke, PhD,** ISTE-certified educator and
professor of education, Commonwealth University of Pennsylvania

"Three central metaphors help readers visualize the functions and purposes of reflection in the learning process. The authors of *Now That I Think About It* have anchored each chapter in research and filled the book with practical classroom examples that will make you want to improve tomorrow's lesson plan with deeper, more meaningful reflections. Students and teachers alike will benefit from this book."

—**Brett Vogelsinger,** teacher, speaker, consultant,
and author of *Artful AI in Writing Instruction*

"Education is shifting away from repetition of conclusions and toward analysis that evaluates whether information is accurate and complete. This book provides reflective tools that emphasize student reasoning, which is an essential skill for developing informed and critical thinkers and will remain so well into this century and the next."

—**Leslie Jasmine Djang, EdD,** assistant principal,
Upper Moreland High School

Now That I Think About It

Now That I Think About It

Teaching Your Students to Be Reflective and Effective Learners

Lynne Dorfman
Catherine Gehman
Pérsida Himmele
Aileen Hower

Arlington, Virginia USA

iste+ascd

2111 Wilson Boulevard, Suite 300 • Arlington, VA 22201 USA
Phone: 800-933-2723 or 703-578-9600
Website: iste-ascd.org • Email: memsupport@iste-ascd.org
Author guidelines: ascd.org/write

Richard Culatta, *Chief Executive Officer;* Genny Ostertag, *Managing Director, Book Acquisitions & Editing;* Bill Varner, *Senior Acquisitions Editor;* Mary Beth Nielsen, *Director, Book Editing & Design;* Katie Martin, *Senior Editor;* Judi Connelly, *Graphic Designer;* Valerie Younkin, *Senior Production Designer;* Cynthia Stock, *Typesetter;* Emily Reed, *Senior Director, Publishing Operations;* Kelly Marshall, *Production Manager;* Christopher Logan, *Senior Production Specialist;* Shajuan Martin, *E-Publishing Specialist*

PAPERBACK ISBN: 978-1-4166-3442-3   Product #125017   m6/26

PDF EBOOK ISBN: 978-1-4166-3443-0; see Books in Print for other formats.

Quantity discounts are available: email programteam@ascd.org or call 800-933-2723, ext. 5773, or 703-575-5773. For desk copies, go to www.ascd.org/deskcopy.

ISTE+ASCD Member Book No. FY26-4. ISTE+ASCD mails member books quarterly (Jan–Mar, Apr–Jun, Jul–Sep, Oct–Dec) with 4 books to Enhanced members and 8 books to Pro members. For current details on membership, see iste-ascd.org/member-books.

Library of Congress Cataloging-in-Publication Data

Names: Dorfman, Lynne R., 1952- author | Gehman, Catherine author | Himmele, Pérsida author | Hower, Aileen author
Title: Now that I think about it : teaching your students to be reflective and effective learners / Lynne Dorfman, Catherine Gehman, Pérsida Himmele, Aileen Hower.
Description: Arlington, Virginia : ISTE+ASCD, [2026] | Includes bibliographical references and index.
Identifiers: LCCN 2026003933 (print) | LCCN 2026003934 (ebook) | ISBN 9781416634423 paperback | ISBN 9781416634430 pdf
Subjects: LCSH: Reflective learning
Classification: LCC LB1027.23 .D67 2026 (print) | LCC LB1027.23 (ebook)
LC record available at https://lccn.loc.gov/2026003933
LC ebook record available at https://lccn.loc.gov/2026003934

35 34 33 32 31 30 29 28 27 26   1 2 3 4 5 6 7 8 9 10 11 12

To teachers everywhere
who nurture a love of learning in their students.

To students everywhere
who courageously explore their own potential
and imagine endless possibilities through reflective practices.

Now That I Think About It

Foreword

On a recent visit to an earth science classroom, I pulled up a chair in the back and sat down next to a 7th grader rummaging through his backpack. "What are you guys working on?" I whispered to him.

He pulled his head out of his bag and whispered back, "I don't really know."

The teacher started class with a question: "What do you all remember about the sun and why we have seasons?"

Silence filled the classroom. Then, from somewhere on the right side of the room: "I don't think you taught that." The teacher sighed and asked the students to take out their science journals.

The kid next to me once again dug into his backpack. "Oh yeah," he said to me. "We are learning about weather."

* * *

We've all been there. We present an amazing lesson. It takes a little longer than we thought. The bell rings, and we pat ourselves on the back for "bell to bell" teaching. The problem is, we didn't leave time, as the experts advise, for students to "zip up the cognitive backpack." It's no wonder students don't remember what we teach when there isn't time to process or reflect.

Reflecting is a lot like meditating or praying—other practices we know are good for us but struggle to find time to do. What's more, not enough of us are explicitly taught *how* to reflect. Just last week, I was conducting a workshop with teachers. At the start, I asked them to reflect on the learning targets. I was surprised, as I increasingly am, when several teachers didn't do it and others were confused by the assignment. "What do you want me to do here?" they asked. I nudged them to ask questions or write down what they were already doing. Some started to jot down words but most just sat there. Like students, a lot of teachers have never been taught how to reflect or given the time to do it.

Reflection takes practice. If you've ever wondered what it means to reflect— I mean, *really* reflect, not just put something on a page to get the workshop presenter out of your face—*Now That I Think About It* is for you. You will become better at reflecting on your practice, and your students will benefit from engaging in the variety of reflection strategies this book provides.

I was hooked early—as soon as I got to the snippet of research about the learning gains students make when they are taught how to reflect. Students whose teachers had built reflection activities into lessons made greater gains than those who practiced the lesson's targeted skills without purposeful reflection. According to the authors and the research they cite, without reflection, little of what we learn moves from theory to effective practice, from test score to real-life application.

If I only had time to teach kids one reading strategy, it would be how to be metacognitive when reading. This book amplifies the power of metacognition, applying it to every aspect of learning. It explicitly shares how teachers can help students be reflective in multiple subject areas. Ahead, you will find protocols and think sheets to guide striving and thriving students. There are ideas for journaling and student samples. There are examples on how to use anchor charts as well as portfolios. Peppered throughout are bits of current cognitive science that provide backing for these strategies and support for dedicating time to reflection. Maybe what strikes me most about this book is how it empowers not only student agency but also teacher agency. Each chapter provides useful discussion questions that can be used with PLCs, student debriefs, and as formative and diagnostic assessments.

I've been waiting for a book like this for a long time. In this fast-paced world where we often find ourselves on autopilot, we need reflection more than ever ... even as we tell ourselves that our overbooked school days and lives don't give us enough time to reflect. Now that I think about it, how do we *not* find time for something so essential?

Cris Tovani
Centennial, Colorado

Introduction

Try to count all the stars in the sky.

Impossible, right?

NASA astronomers estimate there are about a septillion stars scattered throughout the universe. Yet even with access to advanced, complex mathematical calculations, scientists cannot know the exact number of stars in the universe. So why do they keep trying to count them? They do it to gain insight into the complexities and mysteries of the universe.

When we set out to write a book about the complex concept of reflection, it sometimes felt as if we had taken on the task of counting the stars. But we did it anyway. We believe in the value of understanding reflection as an academic practice and making reflection part of every classroom. Why? Because reflection is so powerful, and the insight students can unlock by engaging in it is limitless. Learning can be as unpredictable as the sea. Just as celestial maps once guided ancient sailors in unknown waters, providing them with location and direction, reflection charts a course students can use to navigate their learning. When you think about it, both reflection and the stars can provide guidance; both are invitations to pause, notice, and find a way forward.

This book is a guide to thinking about reflection as a natural and necessary part of learning—not as something difficult or out of reach. For some, this will be a new perspective. When we spoke with classroom teachers during our research, those who did not regularly provide students with opportunities for reflection were not sure how to go about it or where they would find the time. This book answers these questions and more with classroom-ready protocols, practical tips, and relatable classroom snapshots.

We recommend that you begin with Chapter 1 and work your way through the book to experience the intentional flow it has to offer. At the end of each chapter, you'll find discussion prompts and questions, making this a great book to read with your team or to use as a book study for your school or district. Sprinkled throughout the book, you will find QR codes to direct you to short video clips from teachers, administrators, and students. We hope seeing them talk about reflective practices will solidify this work as doable and worth doing as well as provide additional perspectives on how it can be used to enhance teaching and learning. We invite you to begin your own journey of reflection and to use the insight it generates to discover new possibilities for yourself and your students.

1

Why Reflection Matters: Exploring the Role of Reflection in Learning

Life can only be understood backwards; but it must be lived forwards.

—*Søren Kierkegaard*

After listening to a brief presentation peppered with opportunities for guided practice, Mrs. Vargas's students work independently on several math problems at their desks. One of the problems reads as follows:

> Liam wants to buy a new video game that costs $60. The store is having a 30 percent off sale on all video games. Liam has a coupon for $5 off that can be used after the 30 percent deduction is applied. How much will he pay for the video game?

Mrs. Vargas circulates around the room, asking students questions as they work on their solutions. She pauses at Alex's desk and asks him to explain his answer ($13). She doesn't tell Alex the answer is wrong; she wants him to come to that conclusion on his own. Instead, she asks a question: "How did you solve the problem, Alex? Explain for me the steps you took."

Alex begins to talk through his reasoning and calculations: "Thirty percent of $60 is like multiplying .30 times 60, and that gave me 18. Eighteen minus 5 is 13. So, Liam paid $13 for the video game."

Mrs. Vargas looks at him with a faint smile. "Those calculations look right, but I want you to go back and explain this step." She points to where he had multiplied .30 × 60. "Talk me through that."

Alex clarifies, "The .30 is the same as 30 percent. I multiplied 30 percent by 60—the $60—so that gave me $18."

Mrs. Vargas prompts further: "OK, but reread the problem for me."

Alex reads the problem to himself, looking back and forth from the problem to his calculation. "Oh, I see," he says. "Thirty percent *off.* I should have subtracted the $18."

"Why?" asks Mrs. Vargas.

"Because $18 is how much he's *saving*, not what he's paying."

"Perfect! So then, what would your new answer be?"

Alex recalculates with the additional operation and announces the new answer: "Thirty-seven dollars."

Mrs. Vargas offers an affirming fist bump, then continues circulating around the room. She stops to ask students to explain their reasoning as they solve the various problems and celebrates the thinking they share with her. At one point, she pauses at Marisa's desk and says, "Look at all those erasure marks. I love that you're going back and checking your work. That's good thinking!"

Mrs. Vargas does not give quick answers, and she does not immediately point out exactly what students did wrong if there is a mistake. She knows that in this lesson, teaching students to use strategic reflection when choosing mathematical operations is as important as coming up with the right answer. To Mrs. Vargas, there is nothing more satisfying than hearing a student backtrack with a phrase like "Now that I think about it..." or Alex's "OK, I see." For her, this is a sign that real thinking is happening. It tells her a student is strategically reflecting on the question and their answer.

These "aha" moments take place in every subject area when students dig deeper into the content. They mean students are learning to analyze problems or content in ways that produce bigger understandings than they had before. They are facilitated by students talking through their learning, articulating their thinking, and adding to their responses after hearing peers' perspectives. This deep reflection is what we strive for—the way to instill meaningful learning that lasts.

Why Reflection Matters

It's safe to say that little lasting learning takes place without reflection. Reflection engages students in higher-order thinking: analysis, meaning making, and problem solving. It requires students to stop and absorb what has been presented, process what works and what doesn't work in relation to their own learning, and calibrate best approaches to completing a task.

As Porter (2019) puts it, "Reflection gives the brain an opportunity to pause amidst the chaos, untangle and sort through observations and experiences, consider multiple possible interpretations, and create meaning" (p. 39). Pausing to reflect on learning is an essential aspect of processing deeper meaning, but educators must plan for these pauses. The goal of this book is to help educators create these opportunities for reflection and to teach students what to do with them. We aim to explore strategic and visible techniques that will help teachers prompt and guide the act of reflection.

What We Mean by Reflection

Our definition of *reflection is* rooted in research, our lived experiences as classroom teachers, and our own learning journeys:

> Reflection is a deliberate, structured inquiry that moves learners through the complexities of thoughtful examination, giving pause to that which is perplexing, puzzling, and surprising so that the learners can repackage their thinking, create a plan, and move forward in their learning with deeper and more meaningful insights and improved achievement.
>
> Reflection is multifaceted, and in this book, we examine three aspects of it:
>
> **Looking at**—Reflection as a magnifying glass (meaning making)
>
> **Looking in**—Reflection as a mirror (metacognition)
>
> **Looking out**—Reflection as a map (metastrategic thinking)

We'll also examine the role of teacher reflection and important information about learning and the brain.

Reflection as a Magnifying Glass: The Process of Making Meaning

Pamela Kramer Ertel (2021) uses an anecdote to capture the power of reflection. She describes a Monday drive during which she listened to a radio talk show. The host asked churchgoing listeners if they could summarize the sermons they'd heard the day before. Kramer Ertel was surprised to realize that she couldn't: "Although I listened, I neglected to process the meaning and, thereby, just one day later, was unable to recall the message." Considering the implications of this processing failure, she asked herself, "Do my students experience this same inability to recall the main points in my lessons?" (p. 120). Reflection as meaning making requires learners to focus on what is presented or taught to more thoroughly absorb the lesson. It ought to be happening all the time, every day, but it's not likely to do so without teacher intentionality.

To make meaning, students need to follow up on the input they receive from the teacher, texts, and peers by analyzing, summarizing, or in some other way repackaging that input to perform the subsequent task. It requires that students closely examine the lesson to turn out a meaningful product, whether that be a verbal, written, visual, or other type of explanation or analysis. This form of reflection not only ensures that learning has occurred but also provides teachers with visual evidence of the students' learning. Intentionally planning ways for students to demonstrate meaning making increases the likelihood that students will process what they've been taught. Like Kramer Ertel, students who do not engage in the act of reflection are likely to walk away from the lesson unable to recall even its simplest points.

Reflection as a Mirror: The Process of Metacognition

One of the typical non-education-related definitions for reflection is an image projected in a mirror or on a shiny surface. Metacognition, or reflection on one's own learning, is like looking into a metaphorical mirror, and it can be an enlightening and effective method for learning.

Erin Nash (Hallstead & Nash, 2020) wanted to help her first-year university biology students become more proactive about reflecting on their learning. When students scored badly on exams, Nash noticed that they often blamed the professor or attributed the problem to chance (e.g., they had studied the wrong content). Nash decided to survey her students to ascertain habits that led to high and low scores on exams. She placed them in peer groups and analyzed the correlations among reflection behaviors of high score earners. Students who participated in metacognitive reflection processes, or "meta-talks" to improve self-awareness, were more effective learners.

By facilitating students' engagement in healthy reflection, Nash helped them analyze their performance and make productive decisions regarding studying and learning. She and her colleague Tracy Hallstead remind us that "we do not learn through experiences alone; we learn by thinking about our experiences" (p. 103).

Unlike analyzing or processing presented content, at its core, metacognition requires learners to hold up a mirror to focus on their own learning processes and analyze what works best for them and what isn't working. Metacognitive strategies have been shown to be one of the more powerful tools for improving student learning. Hattie (2009) shares that the effect size of metacognition is .6 (effect size tells us how effective a classroom practice is). Psychologists would suggest that an effect size above .5, a medium effect, means that of students who did not participate in the practice of metacognition, over 69 percent scored lower than the mean score of those who were participating, which is a significant outcome. Thinking about their thinking, making decisions based on what they know works, and minimizing what doesn't work provide students with powerful tools and habits for helping them improve their learning.

Reflection as a Map: The Process of Metastrategic Thinking

A third aspect of reflection relates to reflection as a map, or metastrategic thinking: the big-picture evaluation that happens when learners look ahead. Examples of metastrategic thinking include the processes by which learners decide on the best way to complete a task or analyze the implications of newly learned information. It might also look like a learner's reflective pause as they focus on how they might solve a problem, conduct an experiment, effectively construct an argument, write a convincing essay, or draft a moving narrative.

Metastrategic thinking refers to the type of reflection that learners deploy before beginning a task. They look beyond simply completing the task—for example, solving problems with a reader or consumer in mind. Metastrategic reflection is important to advancing society as a whole; it's the type of processing that might generate solutions to address hunger, climate change, and political conflict. It's also the type of thinking that is essential for product design. In an educational context, we see middle school teachers employing metastrategic thinking daily as they navigate the landscape of adolescents' changing emotions, insecurities, and first crushes—all variables that can dramatically affect students' cognitive engagement. In terms of essential attributes of a well-functioning society, metastrategic thinking is a big deal, and there is evidence that we can foster it in our very own classrooms (Iordanou, 2022; Iordanou & Rapanta, 2021; Kuhn et al., 2016; Zohar & Peled, 2008).

Kalypso Iordanou (2022) examined the role of reflection in supporting 6th graders' development of argumentation skills. She found that those who participated in reflection as they practiced argumentation outperformed those who practiced without guided reflection. In her study, 6th graders reflected on their own argumentation, asking themselves whether the evidence they provided made a strong case for their position. They also examined whether they had been able to weaken their opponents' arguments using counterevidence. The students who participated in reflective activities demonstrated more development in metacognition, both as a competence and as a disposition, than their skill-only counterparts. They were also more strategic in their abilities to establish evidence for their position and weaken opposing arguments.

We can support students in the process of thinking ahead by having them reflect on simple prompts like the following as they read or plan projects:

- Why didn't my experiment work?
- What could I have done differently?
- What would happen if I modified it?
- Will this mathematical procedure always work? Why or why not?
- Is this the best/easiest way to solve this problem? Why or why not?
- What is the author's bias?
- What will people who read my essay be thinking as they read it? How will I address that?

In every content area, asking students to dig deeply and analyze implications of what they're learning or producing can lead to metastrategic thinking, with the natural next step of considering how to deal with potential implications. Intentionally structuring our learning to include reflection can foster this type of analysis.

Reflection and the Heart of Teaching

Aside from these three aspects of reflection, this book addresses the benefits of self-reflection for educators. Reflection is at the heart of being a teacher. Although it may go by different names—debriefing, thinking through, connecting with a colleague—reflection is essential to polished teaching (and to life in general). It's the way we process new information, analyze successes so we can repeat them, or dissect conflicts to consider how to handle them differently next time. It's how we engage with professional development, connecting our classroom reality with what we learn in our university courses, books we read, or learning sessions we attend. Without reflection, little of what we learn would move from theory to evidence-based, effective practice.

Multilingual Learners: Reflection as a Check-In Tool

Reflection benefits every student, but it is especially crucial for students learning English as an additional language. In addition to being presented with new content, multilingual learners (MLs) face challenges related to making sense of it in a complex language. Because language is acquired by experiencing and practicing it in contexts we understand, building context around new learning through reflection increases MLs' comprehension of both the content *and* the language.

Incorporating tasks for students to demonstrate their comprehension into your lessons has the added benefit of gathering evidence that MLs are making sense of the learning as it is happening. Be sure to include opportunities for MLs to show you that they are not only comprehending but also going deeper and reflecting on their learning. For example, at the start of using the Jump-Start Reflection Protocol, have students quickly summarize what they have been learning.

Creating a Culture of Reflection

Throughout this book, you'll notice that reading and writing play a critical role in student reflection. Skilled readers use prior knowledge to question, visualize, predict, and apply other reading strategies. The academic day is rife with opportunities to ask students to reflect on the tools, knowledge, and expectations they bring to a science, history, or mathematics text with prompts such as the following:

- *What are you seeing?* (reflection as a magnifying glass)
- *What is working for you, and how do you see yourself growing?* (reflection as a mirror)
- *What will you need to do to be successful?* (reflection as a map)

William Zinsser (1993) describes writing as a powerful tool for thinking aloud on paper. When reflective writing is incorporated into content-area learning, students can write to digest, examine, and analyze the complex content they are learning; reflecting on these processes supports students in truly engaging with and critically consuming content, not just memorizing it to be forgotten later. Assigning students to "think aloud on paper" in a response journal allows teachers to review individual reflections for patterns or generalizations to inform instruction. Questions for reader response in the content areas might include the following:

- *What did you notice in the reading?* (reflection as a magnifying glass)
- *What questions were you asking yourself while you were reading?* (reflection as a mirror)
- *What images were forming in your head that helped you to understand the text?* (reflection as a mirror)
- *What is your plan for successfully reading and understanding the rest of this text?"* (reflection as a map)

At its core, reflection is more than just looking back on learning experiences; it is an intentional, engaging process that deepens understanding, sharpens self-awareness, and guides or affects future decision making. (For a summary of research that supports the power of reflection, see Appendix A.) Reflection creates space for learning to be an active, continuous, and recursive process. In the absence of reflection, there's a risk that learning will become shallow, rote, passive, disconnected, and easily forgotten.

A Teacher's Take

Greg Moll teaches 4th grade math and science at Gilbertsville Elementary in Pennsylvania's Boyertown Area School District. In the linked video, he talks about how his students apply the reflection strategies he's taught them far beyond the classroom. "This isn't just so you get through the math problem," he tells them. "This is for life."

We invite you to read on to explore reflection's role in the learning process in the context of the three primary dimensions—magnifying glass, mirror, and map—that make thinking visible and purposeful.

2

Reflection as a Magnifying Glass: The Process of Making Meaning

Every now and then a [person's] mind is stretched by a new idea or sensation and never shrinks back to its former dimensions.

—Oliver Wendell Holmes

Last spring, Catherine's 4-year-old granddaughter, Sofia, noticed an active ant colony in the yard, near the sky pencil holly. When Catherine and Sofia looked through a magnifying glass, they discovered the ants were carrying what appeared to be some kind of egg. Were these ant eggs? And why were the ants carrying these eggs toward the tree instead of into their hole? The pair had many questions about what the ants were doing.

After some time spent observing the ants, wondering aloud about what they could be up to, remembering ant invasions of childhood picnics (Catherine), and singing "The Ants Go Marching One by One" (Sofia), grandmother and granddaughter embarked on an intense but fun online search and a visit to the public library for books to read. In the process, they made an astonishing discovery: Ants have a symbiotic relationship with aphids. They carry aphid eggs underground for the winter to protect them, and in the spring, they bring these eggs back up to a bush or a tree to hatch. In addition, once the aphids hatch, the ants "milk" them by gently stroking the aphids' bellies with their antennae to help them release honeydew, the waste from the sap that aphids eat. Honeydew is a feast for ants.

Catherine and Sofia's understanding of and appreciation for the common black ant changed that day. Taking a closer look at a specific ant behavior revealed a world of complexities. The experience activated their sensory intake, triggering a search for memories and acquired knowledge to connect with the new input. Just as important, Catherine and Sofia paused to appreciate the ants' tiny yet intricate world and how it relates to our larger one.

The magnifying glass metaphor for reflection reminds us to apply a similar lens to our thinking as we make meaning with new experiences—to zoom in on complex details and then lift our gaze and apply our learning to the broader environment (see Figure 2.1). In this chapter, we explore the transformative power of reflection as a magnifying glass to bring students' thinking into sharper focus. When practiced as an everyday habit, reflection can increase student engagement, deepen understanding, and boost achievement. We also provide simple yet rich protocols that will have a purposeful and lasting effect on student learning.

Figure 2.1

Reflection as a Magnifying Glass: Making Meaning

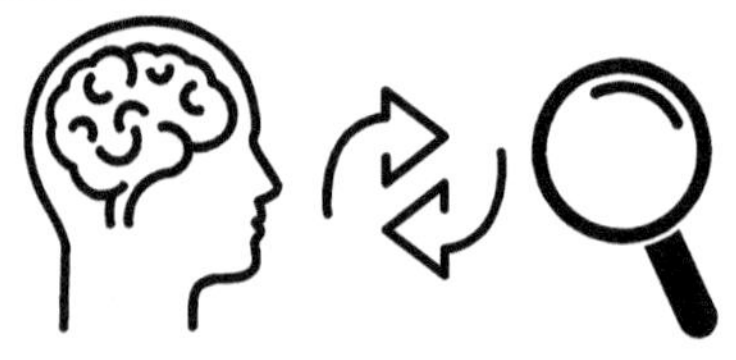

This facet of reflection provides students with opportunities to analyze their learning to connect new content and understandings with previously acquired knowledge.

What Do We Mean by *Making Meaning*?

Making meaning (and *meaning making*; we use the terms interchangeably) refers to how a learner interprets an experience and assigns significance to it. It is an active and ongoing process that begins with a basic awareness of the environment sparked by a sensory experience. The sensory experience is personal to the learner. It might be trying new food, playing a sport, encountering a problem at work, watching a movie, conducting a science experiment, preparing for a debate, tackling a calculus problem or doing long division.... The list is endless. In any case, the learner integrates the new sensory data with previous memories or acquired knowledge, applying the personal lenses of their values, beliefs, and cultural background to form their own interpretation of the new experience's meaning.

Connecting meaning making to reflection is like giving a learner a mental magnifying glass. It positions reflection as a tool that will condition the learner to pause, examine an experience more closely, and uncover insights about it. Trying to make meaning without reflection leads to incomplete or fleeting understanding; it's likely to be surface-level, and it's unlikely to stick. Conversely, with reflection, learning becomes clearer, deeper, and lasting.

In *The Whole-Brain Child* (2012), Siegel and Bryson offer this explanation of how the brain makes meaning:

> When we have a new experience or concentrate on something—say, on how we feel or a goal we'd like to achieve—that activates neural firing. In other words, neurons (our brain cells) spring into action. This neural firing leads to the production of proteins that enable new connections to be wired among the activated neurons. Remember, neurons that fire together wire together. This entire process—from neural activation to neural growth and strengthened connections—is *neuroplasticity*. Essentially, it means that the brain itself is plastic, or changing, based on what we experience, and what we give our attention to. And these new neural connections, created when we pay attention to something, in turn alter the way we respond to and interact with our world. This is how practice can become a skill and how a state can become a trait, for good or for bad. (p. 99)

Reflection, attention, and focus are all components of learning. Each reinforces the others to deepen understanding and increase retention. As King and Tran (2017) write, "To aid in full understanding of especially the more complex ideas, learners benefit from opportunities to externalize and reflect on their thinking. Externalizing is the written or verbal articulation of one's evolving understanding, which allows learners the opportunity to share their unformed ideas with others" (p. 69). When we give students the time and tools to reflect, we ignite the process of neural firing in their brains. Reflection turns meaning making into an intentional and consistent habit that strengthens both the brain and the learning that occurs within it.

Why a Magnifying Glass?

The first documented use of a magnifying lens dates to the days of Roman philosopher Seneca, who is said to have filled a glass globe with water to make letters appear larger. In the 13th Century, Roger Bacon developed a more refined version of the magnifying glass, similar to the one we know today. Once called a "flea glass" for its ability to make even the tiniest details visible, the magnifying glass became one of the most important instruments in history through its impact on science and medicine.

Like reflection itself, the magnifying glass is a simple tool with profound power. It employs no artificial, distorting filters or distractions; it doesn't alter what it's examining in any way. It simply allows the observer to see an object differently and more accurately. There's nothing magical about a magnifying glass, even though its effect can seem magical—perhaps because, in this hurried world, it helps us slow down to take notice of what has been there all along. Maybe slowing down in this way invites wonder, making us feel suspended in time; think of children exemplifying unhurried wonder when they stop to watch an earthworm muscle its way back into the soil or when they can't take their gaze off a lightning bug in a jar. Observing with a magnifying glass also brings clarity, enhancing our ability to see fine details invisible to the naked eye. In the classroom, positioning reflection as a magnifying glass helps students find clarity and gain insight. As they pause to think about new learning, they often find themselves saying, "Oh, I didn't see that before!" When we give students the time to reflect, looking beneath the surface of their learning to make meaning, they find themselves saying, "Now I get it!"

Another reason that a magnifying glass is a powerful metaphor for reflection is that both are practical, enduring tools. The simple convex lens attached to a handle—like the one you probably have in a drawer somewhere—has remained relatively unchanged in form since medieval times because it still works! Like a magnifying glass, reflection is a low-cost, high-impact classroom tool. It manifests its practical and enduring nature when teachers provide time and space before, during, or after a lesson for the students to ask themselves, *How does this connect to what I already know? What's working? What's not working? How will I clear up confusion? What do I need to do to move forward?* Reflection can make a difference in the level of success students experience in their educational (and personal) life.

Students who actively use reflection tools such as sentence stems, journaling, protocols, or lesson-targeted questions are not learning passively but forming stronger neural pathways. Just as a magnifying glass becomes transformational when we pick it up and look through its lens, so does reflection enhance learning when students purposefully engage and take ownership. The magnifying glass, like reflection, is a timeless tool rich with possibilities.

When a Lesson Doesn't Stick

Greg was preparing to teach his science class a new concept. He meticulously planned his lesson as always. Based on the high level of student questions and engagement when he taught it, he was sure the lesson would stick in his students' minds. The next day, he began the class with a short review, expecting to move quickly into his next lesson. Instead, the students met him with silence and blank stares. It was as if everything they had learned the day before had vanished—valuable content was swept away like dust in a gust of wind.

We can all relate to Greg's experience. When lessons don't "stick," even in the face of highly effective and experienced educators' best efforts, it's normal for teachers to question themselves and reflect on *why* it didn't stick. Typically, they focus on their own performance and what they missed or didn't do well. *Was the lesson clear enough?* they ask themselves. *Did I answer questions thoroughly? Was I too this, too that?* After all, teachers are trained to engage in critical self-reflection.

While this type of self-reflection *is* essential to improving educational practice, the responsibility for a lesson failing to stick may not fully lie with the teacher but rather with whether students had the time, space, and skill to engage in reflection themselves. Without that necessary pause to hold up a magnifying glass to their thinking, students gain only fleeting impressions instead of lasting understanding. They need time and space to zoom in—to examine what they are learning, what makes sense, and what is still confusing or puzzling them. Missing that step keeps them from being able to "repackage" their learning for later retrieval.

Classroom Snapshot: Math Concepts with Digital Storytelling

When Catherine informed her 4th grade class that they would be creating digital stories, the students' eyes lit up, and they began to eagerly exchange ideas. But there was a surprising twist: Catherine asked the students to create "teaching stories" based on a math concept they had recently learned.

After arranging the students into groups of two or three, she laid out guidelines for the project: create a storyboard, write a script, and digitize the story using Google Vids. The students found that interpreting a math concept using a new digital platform was more challenging than they had expected. They needed to rely on one another's strengths as they worked toward the goal of sharing a polished video with the class.

Catherine introduced the Magnifying Glass Reflection Protocol (Appendix B) to her students. It's not uncommon for students to plow through assignments without stopping to reflect, and this protocol offers structured support to encourage them to slow down and make sense of their learning when they encounter obstacles. She gave them the protocol in advance and explained how to use it, allowing them the freedom to apply it to moments that felt meaningful to them.

Catherine noticed Liam sitting quietly and gazing around while other students were progressing. His partner had been absent all week, so he was working independently on the project and struggling to move to the planning stage. Sensing he was at a standstill, she suggested the protocol. Liam's reflections are recorded in Figure 2.2.

Note that Liam's responses to questions 3 and 4 illustrate his transition from being stuck on the problem to making a plan to overcome it. He realized he was struggling to choose a story topic among "so many options" and decided falling back on a familiar experience (*beachgoing*) would be a good tactic.

In between answering these questions, he had sought advice from another group about his struggle to decide how to move forward. After implementing the protocol, he was able to continue working with more ease and certainty.

When Catherine asked students about the usefulness of the protocol, their responses were revealing:

> **Student 1:** I think there is value for kids because they can think back on the good and bad.
> **Student 2:** When I paused to reflect, I learned that instead of just rushing ahead and focusing on getting it done, I must put in more effort and try in the future to fix mistakes.
> **Student 3:** I think it helps to untangle and solve problems, control emotions, and so much more.

The digital storytelling assignment concluded with a viewing celebration for the class, at which it was clear the project was a huge success—in part because students took the time to reflect on their learning.

Figure 2.2

Liam's Responses to the Magnifying Glass Reflection Protocol for the Digital Storytelling Project

<table>
<tr>
<td>

Instructions
Name three things in your learning that are difficult, confusing, or a roadblock in your learning right now. Use these sentence starters if you need help:

- I am stuck on . . .
- I can't figure out . . .
- My thinking is tangled up with . . .

1. *Learning how to use Google Vids*

2. *Planning* 

3. *Removing background*

Place a star (★) next to the most challenging one and reflect in the box on the right.

</td>
<td>

Which problem did you star?
____

Reflect on this problem by answering the questions below:

1. Describe the learning experience.

Creating a digital story based on a math concept

2. For this learning experience, what is going well or makes the most sense to you?

What's going well is creating the characters

3. What doesn't make sense? Where is your thinking tangled? How do you feel about it?

I am struggling with creating a story that pleases me because there are so many options and I don't know what to pick

4. What plan will you make to untangle your thinking so you can understand and move forward? Will you get help from a peer? Will you look for examples? Will you find a tutorial? Or will you find a different solution?

I am going to untangle my thinking by trying to do something that I have experienced before like going to the beach

Now that you have reflected on your learning experience, return to your problem and work through the hard parts. When you are finished, record what you did and how well it worked on the back of this sheet.

</td>
</tr>
</table>

Reflection is a powerful bonding agent between new information and understanding that lasts. When students reflect, their brains engage in powerful change:

> All learning (changes in knowledge or skills) results from physical changes to the brain. *Neuroplasticity* is the process by which, after repeated use, newly formed short-term memories can become

> long-term memories. Neuroplasticity permits extensive interconnection of the brain cells. It allows memory information to be efficiently stored, conducted, and rapidly retrieved when needed. The result is like that of multilane expressways, which allow more and faster traffic. (Willis & Willis, 2020, p. 115)

These metaphorical expressways cannot form if students lack curiosity and awareness connected with pausing to be curious and noticing what's important. Like a magnifying glass, reflection is only useful when teachers put it in students' hands. Reflection is the key that opens the door to curiosity and awareness. (See Appendix C for a teaching resource about the brain.)

Multilingual Learners: Using Reflection to Revisit, Retrieve, and Repackage Content

As mentioned earlier, reflection is crucial for all student learning, but it is especially important for multilingual learners (MLs). Listening in one's "weaker" language requires work that can take a toll on comprehension. When we ask students to revisit, retrieve, and repackage content, they have to first go back and focus on whatever they missed, make sense of it, and then articulate the most important and interesting aspects of the lesson. It's a process that solidifies their comprehension of the material and helps make it their own. MLs—who are often exhausted by the effort required to make literal sense of the words they're hearing or on the page—benefit hugely from this kind of reflection.

Reflection Protocols to Cultivate Deeper Meaning

Access to meaningful protocols makes it more likely that students will move past surface-level ideas to get to deep, creative, meaningful thinking. They help students make sense of new information immediately and support memory formation (Alberini & Kandel, 2014). The beauty of these scaffolded tools is that once you guide students through them, students can access them digitally or on paper and apply them to future lessons.

This section highlights reflection routines developed by teachers and researchers to guide and scaffold students' thinking, to make reflection *visible* to students and their teachers, and to help students internalize reflection as a habit. These tools are useful in many different settings, and we have organized them into three categories for ease of navigation: reflection protocols to cultivate deeper meaning, reflection strategies that make learning stick, and reflecting with digital tools.

The Question Formation Technique (QFT) Protocol

We ask our students questions for a wide variety of reasons: to spark a discussion, deepen meaning, ignite curiosity, clarify understanding, bring about higher-order thinking, and more. Intentional questioning opens pathways of thinking that may not exist otherwise. However, consider this: When it comes to questioning, the power lies in the one who asks the questions. What if we place that power in the hands of students? How would we do that? Of the many effective questioning tools we've seen and used in the classroom, the QFT Protocol is one of the best. This eight-step technique guides students to reflect on a specific focus and generate and revise questions related to that focus. After some practice, the QFT Protocol can be used by a student or group of students without a facilitator. Step-by-step instructions for this technique appear in Appendix D.

The Sticky Note Reflection Pathway Protocol

When students struggle to move beyond surface-level ideas, they must learn the essential skill of elaboration. The Sticky Note Reflection Pathway Protocol is a great tool to support this learning. After taking in new information—watching a video, reading an article, conducting an experiment, or the like—students record their impressions on three separate sticky notes. They may record a word, phrase, sentence, or question. Following a brief, small-group discussion to share what they wrote, each student chooses their "weakest" sticky note. They are then guided through a series of questions to expand their thinking. Students are often surprised when they compare their initial response to their final one. Appendix E contains the Sticky Note Reflection Pathway form and facilitator guidelines.

Classroom Snapshot: Noticing Details and Making Connections

It's not unusual for students to read a text and walk away without giving themselves a chance to think critically, notice nuances, or connect the reading to their own life. Many students read on grade level but miss the opportunity to discover the depth of meaning that the author intended. Whether they are striving readers or thriving readers, all students can benefit from the use of reflection protocols to make reflection an academic habit.

Millie was one of Catherine's 4th grade students. She showed enthusiasm for recommended books and displayed a positive attitude in class. Although Millie also performed well on reading assessments, she struggled to focus during independent reading time—whispering, repositioning herself, leaving for the bathroom, or peering around the room. On a reading inventory, Millie indicated that she could not enjoy reading if there were distractions, so reading in school was difficult. She revealed that she didn't read for pleasure over summer break and also noted that she could picture her favorite books in her head but couldn't recall their names.

Catherine's first step to improve Millie's reading life was to ensure she had material that was a good fit. When that didn't help, Catherine started looking for other obstacles. When she analyzed Millie's reading notebook, a pattern emerged: The entries were short and focused on Millie's feelings about a character or situation. This matched her verbal responses in group discussions, which showed strong empathy, but Millie often missed details that could lead to deeper thinking. To assist Millie, Catherine decided to take her through the Sticky Note Reflection Pathway Protocol (Appendix E).

After reading *Eleven* by Sandra Cisneros aloud, Millie wrote down three thoughts about the short story:

1. *I feel sorry and bad because it's her birthday and everything is just going wrong.*
2. *When I am having a bad day, I just can't wait till it's lunch like Rachel did.*
3. *I would feel excited if I was Rachel because you're turning 11, like how I felt excited when I turned 10.*

Following the protocol, Millie chose Thought Number 2 to strengthen. With guidance, she revised and expanded her thinking:

> *When I am having a bad day, I just can't wait till it's lunch like Rachel. In my opinion, Rachel just felt bad because everybody was just being mean. They were saying the red sweater was hers when it wasn't. What's important about this is you can't always assume things. A quote from the text says, "'I think it belongs to Rachel,' Sylvia says, and the teacher says, 'Of course it's yours.'" That shows those two people assumed things—even on her birthday—to make it worse.*

Millie made a connection with the text about a disappointing birthday she had the year before and remained at the table to share her experience with Catherine. That is how a simple protocol led to deeper writing, authentic conversation, and a meaningful connection to a text.

The Neuro-Reflection Protocol

Allowing learners to pause and reflect on a new experience helps them identify and address obstacles in their learning so they can forge ahead with confidence. And when they can recognize and articulate these obstacles well, they are far more likely to repeat the strategies that worked for them. The Neuro-Reflection Protocol (see Appendix F) is a five-step process that gives students space to practice with this type of reflection. Learners begin by using a Likert-like scale to rate the amount of previous experience they have with a skill or concept and their perception of the difficulty level of the learning. They continue by engaging in four open-ended prompts. Facilitated by a teacher, the Neuro-Reflection Protocol provides unique insights into student thinking and learning. Chapter 3 addresses this protocol further.

The 5Rs Reflection Framework Protocol

Moving beyond recall to critical thinking is one of the greatest challenges students face in reflecting on their learning. The 5Rs Reflection Framework Protocol (Bain et al., 2002; see Appendix G) provides a structured approach to meaningful reflection, guiding students to report, respond, relate, reason, and reconstruct. The focus of the protocol can be academic or personal, and the process can be guided by a facilitator or completed independently.

The What? So What? Now What? Protocol

This simple yet effective model takes participants through three basic phases of reflection at any point during a learning experience. It is designed to be used across content areas and with all ages (extra support may be needed for younger students). The What? So What? Now What? Protocol (Borton, 1970; see Appendix H) helps individuals derive meaning from an experience and explore how to move forward by posing three questions:

1. **What?**—Describe the experience by explaining the context, facts, and feelings involved.
2. **So What?**—Find meaning by thinking about theories to help make sense of the experience.

3. **Now What?**—Focus on creating an action plan based on responses to the previous questions.

Reflection Strategies That Make Learning Stick

The reflection strategies in this section are connected in several ways. For the most part, they have a combined ability to enhance memory, comprehension, and creative expression through multimodal learning practices. These techniques complement the cognitive benefits of interleaving through engaging methods for information processing and personal reflection. Strategies such as sketchnoting, digital storytelling, and digital journals represent applied methods of active learning and multimodal expression that can facilitate the cognitive benefits of interleaving

Interleaving

Traditionally, teaching students new information or skills involves introducing the lesson and then practicing the same strategy or type of problem until students achieve mastery (or give up). However, working on several different types of problems or topics in a single study session or practice period—an approach called *interleaving*—makes it more likely that the brain will retain the new information or skills long-term (Rohrer & Taylor, 2010). A simple example would be a student math assignment that alternates sets of problems among two-digit multiplication, two-digit division, and multistep problems that combine both, as opposed to an assignment that assesses only two-digit multiplication. The concepts are related, but the first assignment increases retention for the student.

Interleaving is effective because the brain responds well to variety. Interleaving strengthens the ability to distinguish between concepts, forging stronger neural pathway connections. Moreover, it promotes cognitive flexibility, forcing the brain to adapt. The shift in attention to different concepts requires effort, which leads to deeper understanding, which leads to better and longer learning retention. The traditional "block" approach to practicing a lot of the same thing can be beneficial for the short term, but interleaving has a more robust effect for the long term (Rohrer & Taylor, 2010).

"Dend-Write" Prompts

Dend-write prompts—a play on words regarding the neural cell structure known as a *dendrite*—guide students to summarize and consolidate new learning (Willis & Willis, 2020). Such prompts can be posted for students to choose from for an end-of-day reflection journal entry or for a standalone assignment. Here are some examples:

- One thing I learned today is...
- One thing that surprised me today was...
- Something I'd like to find out more about is...
- Something that confused me is...
- A question I have is...

Students' responses to these types of prompts make the learning they acquired that day visible to the teacher, serving as formative assessment data that a teacher can use to guide future instruction, as well as foster improved communication between teacher and students.

Sketchnoting

Sketchnoting—taking notes in a format that combines words and drawings—is an enjoyable way for students to take ownership of new learning. They can use speech bubbles, thought bubbles, doodles, and so on to capture new concepts in ways that make sense to them, based on their prior knowledge and experiences. Sketchnoting requires learners to listen, think, and synthesize—not just record the teacher's words. The process of choosing which images they will sketch helps them organize their thoughts. Sketchnoting also asks students to think spatially and use metacognitive skills to plan how to fill the page—two additional elements of meaning making—to form their own personal interpretations and connections.

Writing Newspaper Columns

One way to engage students in reflective work that solidifies understanding is to ask them to take on the role of a newspaper columnist writing about what they are learning. For example, a student studying the civil rights moment might pretend to be a columnist in 1955 Montgomery, Alabama, writing about Rosa Parks's quiet act of defiance and how the Montgomery Bus Boycott is igniting change by showing the power of peaceful protest. Introducing this reflective, evaluative element—the requirement that students form an opinion and back it up—helps to deepen their understanding and spurs them to clarify anything they don't grasp. They also build empathy as they think "beyond the facts" and contemplate such questions as *What would I have done in that situation?* or *Would I be that courageous?* or *If Rosa were alive today, what would she think about the world as it is now?*

Reflecting with Digital Tools

Digital tools, when used with intentionality and caution, can help students build the habit of reflection.

Because the potential for distraction that accompanies technology use can undercut students' intention to partake in meaningful reflection, it's important to provide user guidelines that mitigate risks, which range from time-stealing "doomscrolling" to exposure to cyberbullying to unhealthy comparison with others. When teachers build students' capacity to introspectively analyze the effect the digital world has on them and to examine how they can choose to use devices more to learn and less to derive instant gratification, they create a beautiful, tension-filled, exciting possibility that students can grow in ways they never imagined.

Digital Storytelling

We love stories—partly because, at the end of reading or hearing a story, our brains trigger the release of dopamine, the neurotransmitter associated with pleasure, reward, and motivation. Writing stories to reflect on how we learn or make meaning can be both enjoyable and an effective way to make learning stick. It allows the learner to reconstruct learned facts and mentally manipulate them to gain a stronger understanding (Willis & Willis, 2020). Learning anchored in a meaningful context, such as a story, may also help trigger biological responses that stabilize memory, greatly improving the chances of the learning experience moving from fragile short-term impressions to long-term understanding (Alberini, 2014).

Digital storytelling is a powerful way for students to combine visual, auditory, and narrative elements to create compelling accounts to showcase a learning experience. It facilitates the transformation of traditional teaching practices by providing opportunities for students to construct knowledge, express creativity, and develop digital literacy skills. One example is a math student creating a short teaching video with characters he has digitally brought to life to explain how to plot and interpret points on a coordinate plane.

Digital storytelling using platforms such as Powtoon (www.powtoon.com) and Animoto (https://animoto.com) accommodates a range of learning preferences and styles by combining multimedia elements such as text, voice, and images. It also promotes communication and teamwork as students share ideas and helpful criticism (Tamimi, 2024).

Blogging

Blogging allows students to revisit their learning experience in an engaging way by providing the motivating component of an authentic audience. It requires the learner to pause and conceptualize how to communicate what they know about a topic in a clear, concise way. Bloggers are not limited to expository writing; they can also craft poetry, create doodle fiction, conduct interviews, and more to showcase their understanding. The comment feature adds a collaborative element that can validate the learner and instill confidence.

Podcasting

To create an effective podcast, instead of reciting facts about what they've learned, students must make key decisions about what matters most in the content and how to communicate it to the listener. This requires employing higher-order thinking skills. There are many online tools and tutorials for teachers to choose from to support podcasting. Podcasts allow students to feel like professional communicators, reaching out to an authentic audience, which makes learning meaningful and authentic. Moreover, it provides a creative outlet that can enhance traditional learning.

Digital Journals

A digital journal is a technological platform for students to record their thoughts and reflections on learning. Unlike a publicly accessible blog, a digital journal is a more personal space meant for only the learner, the learner and the teacher, or a small group. The format offers a consistent, low-pressure process for students to record their thinking, evaluate their growth, set goals, or track progress over time. Students especially enjoy the ability to incorporate images, videos, links, and voice recordings to enrich their reflection.

It's not uncommon for students to journal as if they are writing in a personal diary. Kelly Gallagher (2011) brings light to this by explaining the difference between expressive writing and reflective writing. He explains that good reflective writing goes beyond giving an account of the past, bringing new insight. Although both expressive and reflective writing can relate to any subject area, it's essential—if challenging—to help students move from expressive writing to reflective writing. Modeling the process for students is key.

Appendix I delves into the difference in the types of writing and offers examples in several content areas.

Final Thoughts on Reflection as a Magnifying Glass

We are teachers. Even with our best efforts, there are days when things don't go well for our students. That goes without saying. But when we teach our students to pick up a metaphorical magnifying glass, it gives them the agency they need and crave as they make meaning of experiences and shape their learning journey. We've heard the saying "Whoever is doing the talking is doing the learning." What if we apply this same line of thinking to reflection: "Whoever is doing the *reflecting* is doing the learning"?

In our daily planning, as we make key pedagogical decisions, let's move reflection from the back burner to the front by making it an everyday habit. Let's teach students how their brains make meaning so they can become more self-aware learners, and we can become more compassionate, empathetic teachers. Doing so sets our students up for success in a world that requires higher-order, creative thinking. Let's shift from the frantic "do, do, do" to "do, pause, reflect, untangle, do"—a much-needed change—to help our students find value in owning their learning. Reflection is key to unlocking a world for themselves and others in which they not only live but thrive.

For those who embrace the process, reflection as meaning making sets the foundation for deeper understanding and opens the mind to new possibilities and lasting learning.

Questions for Individual Reflection

1. How can the metaphor of reflection as a magnifying glass help your students take ownership of their learning?
2. What practical tool will you try in your classroom soon?
3. What questions are still lingering for you about meaning making through reflection?
4. What gives you pause about thinking about reflection as a magnifying lens. How have you/can you overcome this?
5. When your students think about reflection as a magnifying lens, what observable connections do you see them making between their learning and personal experiences?

Questions to Discuss with Colleagues

1. Where could you apply the metaphor of reflection as a magnifying glass into your work across content areas?
2. Discuss your understanding of the following statement and how it can inform your teaching practice: "Reflection is a powerful bonding agent between new information and understanding that lasts. When students reflect, their brains engage in powerful change."
3. Discuss how using reflection for meaning making is related to higher-order thinking skills.
4. How can you apply the concept of reflection as a magnifying glass to encourage your students to be more active learners?
5. Describe a learning experience for which students produced a written reflection and talk about it with colleagues. Which skills helped your students with the learning process?
6. How can reflection as a magnifying glass best serve your students?

3

Reflection as a Mirror: Metacognitive Thinking

> *Metacognition is more than simple reflection: it's an internal dialogue between self as thinker and self as learner. Self-regulated learners are metacognitively, motivationally, and behaviorally active participants in their own learning.*
>
> *—Barry J. Zimmerman*

While guiding a writing lesson with 3rd grade students, Aileen tapped into metacognitive strategies to increase its effectiveness. The class was discussing the difference between what was important versus what was interesting in a text about the blue morpho butterfly.

As they read the first page of the text together ("Did you see that flash of blue in the forest..."), one of the students started to write that sentence under the "important" category. Aileen stopped to ask why he thought that was important information. He replied, "It's the first line of the book, so it must be important."

Aileen responded by asking all the students to put themselves into the mind of a writer or to think back to their writing classes. "When you are choosing what to write to catch your reader's attention," she said, "do you start with an important fact or something 'interesting' to help your reader become interested in what you are writing about?" The first student used his metacognitive skills (i.e., thinking about his thinking) to both recognize the problem and actively adjust his comprehension strategy. He listed the first line under "interesting" instead.

What Do We Mean by *Metacognitive Reflection*?

Metacognition occurs when we think about what and how we are thinking. In other words, we reflect on the thoughts that go into our learning. This could mean reflecting on the steps we take to solve a math equation—articulating verbally or in writing the thoughts that led us to the solution. It could look like reflecting on what is going through our mind when we listen to a read-aloud—what prior knowledge we have, what connections we are making, and how we are confirming or adjusting what we know as we listen to and interact with the text.

Perhaps metacognition is best exemplified by a teacher performing a "think-aloud" as they model for students what they are thinking as they interact with a learning activity. The teacher might read a portion of the text, verbalize what questions they have or ideas they are generating, and recount the actions they will take. All these steps help make learning "visible" to students, which is a powerful tool for facilitating student reflection.

Why a Mirror?

One of the common definitions of *reflection* is an image projected in a mirror or shiny surface. Metacognition, or reflection on one's own learning, is like looking into a metaphorical mirror—an enlightening and effective way to process learning (see Figure 3.1).

Figure 3.1

Reflection as a Mirror: Metacognition

Zimmerman (2002) emphasizes the importance of self-regulated learning to academic success. In his studies, he found that students who actively engaged in self-monitoring and self-evaluation were significantly more likely to perform well academically. Rather than attributing poor performance to external factors like unfair tests or inadequate instruction, these students developed the ability to assess their own study habits and adjust them accordingly. Similarly, a study by Tanner (2012) highlights the effectiveness of metacognitive prompts in biology classrooms. When reflective questions such as *What strategies did I use to prepare for this exam?* or *What might I do differently next time?* were embedded into coursework, students became more aware of their cognitive processes. These reflections encouraged learners to take ownership of their academic development, fostering a shift from passive reception to active engagement in learning.

Metacognition goes beyond recalling what was learned to examine how learning takes place. It requires students to step outside the content and consider their approach to it. Like scrutinizing themselves in a mirror, learners can evaluate their thinking strategies, assess their effectiveness, and explore alternatives when necessary.

Research supports the power of these strategies. According to Donohoo and colleagues (2018), metacognitive strategies yield a high-impact effect size of 0.69 on student achievement. In educational research, this effect size suggests that students who engage in metacognitive practices significantly outperform their peers who do not. These findings reinforce the idea that helping students develop the habit of thinking about their thinking can lead them to be more strategic, independent, and successful learners. By fostering reflective practices in the classroom, educators equip students with lifelong tools for learning—not just to perform better on exams but to develop into more capable, self-aware, problem-solving individuals.

Multilingual Learners: Using Reflection to Take Ownership of Their Learning

Metacognitive reflection plays a critical role for all students, but it is especially important for multilingual learners, to whom school can often feel like a deluge of content that is easy to tune out. Focusing on metacognition signifies to MLs the importance of taking an active role in their own learning by understanding what works for them and how to capitalize on metacognitive strategies. It can be empowering to understand that there are things that you can do and strategies you can employ to become a more effective learner, particularly for those who feel that much of the learning day is controlled by others. Metacognitive scaffolds can also provide teachers with a window into what is being learned, an opportunity to celebrate growth, and a pathway toward what's still needed. Awakening multilingual learners to the powerful role they can play in their own learning journey will have lifelong benefits that far outlast the lesson being taught.

Types of Metacognition

Sajna Jaleel (2016) describes metacognition, reflection as a mirror to examine one's own thoughts, as having two components: (1) thinking about one's thinking and learning processes, which we have been discussing, and (2) self-regulation, in which students consider how they participate in learning. "Developing these metacognitive abilities is not simply about becoming reflective learners," she notes, "but about acquiring specific learning strategies as well.... Questions that explicitly help students think about *How do I study best?* or *What kinds of tools help me learn?* all engage metacognitive knowledge" (p. 165). Ultimately, she writes, students need to be able to do the following:

- Accurately understand and evaluate their knowledge and skills in a subject;
- Monitor their learning and strategy use;
- Think about how to be flexible in their approach to learning, shifting to a different strategy or method of learning when they recognize one is not working for them;
- Work efficiently, knowing whether to focus on main ideas or details as warranted;
- Note which strategies and skills help them achieve mastery; and
- Consistently test their knowledge to see if their strategies are working and that they are retaining the concepts they are studying (Sajna Jaleel, 2016).

Including metacognitive strategies and routines throughout lessons will increase students' confidence. Additionally, metacognitive strategies and routines anchor students' abilities to problem-solve during learning and promote their capacity to implement strategies to foster their own learning.

In *Smart but Scattered* (2008), Peg Dawson and Richard Guare classify metacognition as an advanced executive skill due to the role it plays in problem solving. Advanced executive skills can take until age 24 to fully develop, so providing students with many opportunities for practice, especially guided practice in earlier grades—is advisable. Opportunities to participate in metacognitive reflection helps students become more strategic learners throughout their upper elementary, secondary, and college years.

Metacognitive reflection slows a student down and calls their attention to how they have been thinking about and interacting with and within the world. When teachers help students pause to reflect, students can more readily transfer their new learning to other contexts and integrate it with concepts they have mastered. By examining their own thought processes, they can find ways to move forward, to change, or to create something new and better. They begin to understand their strengths and identify areas that need some work.

Metacognitive reflection is internal and student driven. And it can be messy and unpredictable because it is change created from the inside. But in the end, because it brings insights into why learning is or isn't effective, it effects a more lasting change.

Classroom Snapshot: Metacognition with the Neuro-Reflection Protocol

"Hello, mathematicians!" Greg greeted his students. The class had been working hard on story problems using a tape diagram—a visual tool that represents relationships between numbers. Greg explained that today's math class would conclude with a reflection using the Neuro-Reflection Protocol (see Appendix F). The goal was for them to step back and observe their thought processes, identify where they made progress, determine where they struggled, evaluate their growth, and connect their learning to the world beyond school.

Bella's and Ethan's responses to the protocol's worksheet prompts (see Figure 3.2) provide powerful insight into how two learners from different backgrounds think about their learning. Bella faces academic challenges in reading and math, while Ethan participates in the gifted program and excels in academic subjects. Both are highly creative thinkers. A look at their reflections illustrates that metacognitive reflection is valuable for *all* learners because it fosters a growth mindset and cultivates self-awareness and emotional regulation.

Figure 3.2

Example: Bella and Ethan's Responses to the Neuro-Reflection Protocol Prompts

Prompt	Bella's Response	Ethan's Response
One brain muscle I built today:	*It was challenge when thar was multy tasck things* • *When i had to make a tape diagrame* • *I have trouble when I have to finnout if I have a to sbutracte*	• I just blocked everything out. • I imagined what if it would look right.
Thinking that was hard or got tangled up for me in this lesson, and how I felt about it:	*It is hard to remember to label* • *It is hard when I get disstractid* • *I felt upset when I got it rong*	• Remembering to add the extra one • Adding extra labels so I know what is what
One thing I appreciate about how this lesson helped me grow:	*I felt prode when I got a 20/24 on my test I knew I was growing and I was happy*	I am proud of being able to add tons of different parts at once and get an exact answer.
How knowing this skill or concept adds value to my life:	*It helps me with my homework like my parints make me do extra homewark*	Slowing down helps me understand being patients and calmness, so now I can wait calmly.

Despite differences in their life experiences and academic levels, both Bella and Ethan successfully articulated their thinking. Bella embraced the pride she felt in her test performance and could see value in her learning. Ethan's responses revealed his growth in strategic thinking and emotional self-regulation.

The Neuro-Reflection Protocol guides students to reflect on both their struggles and their successes, helping to make learning feel more meaningful. Reflection like this nudges students to take ownership of their process, connect what they've learned to the real world, and recognize their growth.

Classroom Strategies for Reflection as a Mirror

Successful readers are metacognitive. They plan their reading, monitor and evaluate it, and move forward. They are motivated and engaged. As Afflerbach and colleagues (2013) point out, metacognition contributes to reading comprehension by making students aware of their own thinking processes. It helps them to understand what they need to learn and how to implement cognitive strategies, skills, and the learning process. Their 2013 article in *The Reading Teacher* lists teacher questions that model metacognition for students, such as "Can I get back on track?" (p. 443); teacher questions on a student reading checklist, such as "I try to maintain my reading, even when I encounter problems" (p. 443); and a corresponding metacognitive action. Tools like this can help both teachers and students scaffold initial work to foster metacognitive thinking until such processes are automatic and internalized for ready use.

In Kevin Bower's 6th grade class, metacognitive activities are used throughout each lesson to facilitate learning and improve student engagement. Co-teacher Josey Dombach asks students to think metacognitively about the learning that they are completing or have just finished. The pair have been known to ask students to "talk as a team about how you think the builders created the treehouse with such interesting shapes" while technology loads. While waiting for other groups to finish, students in a grammar lesson have been directed to "discuss how to use commas and quotation marks to help writers strengthen their writing and create diverse sentences." In science class, during group work, students were directed to create a machine to extract a core sample of a potato standing in for a space rock. "Students worked and talked together to create their tool," they report. "Then they talked through and problem-solved how to make adjustments until they obtained a clean sample." Engaging in metacognition is a natural part of the course that enables the class to participate in game-based, project-based, or activity-focused learning activities as opposed to more lecture-based, worksheet-focused learning.

Let's look at some of the ways teachers can get more metacognition into students' day-to-day learning.

Verbal Reflection and Quick-Writes

At the end of a day's lesson, or even at strategic moments throughout the lesson, teachers can guide students to reflect on how they are learning, either verbally or through a quick-write. Here are some prompt suggestions for questions students can ask themselves:

- *What am I learning?*
- *What might I be missing?*
- *What is working for me in this lesson?*
- *What is not working for me in this lesson?*
- *What is the most important thing I learned today?*
- *What did I appreciate most about my learning today?*
- *What do I want/need to learn more about?*

These questions focus on the student's learning rather than on what the teacher is or isn't doing. They shift the role of the teacher back to guide-on-the-side instead of sage-on-the-stage. So much of the conversation around educators in upper grades is about what teachers are (or are not) doing for students to get them to learn. But that's not how learning works. Metacognitive reflection requires the learner to be active, notice what role they are (or are not) playing in the classroom, and think about what they are thinking about the topic. This allows them to invest in themselves, be curious, and contribute their thoughts to discussions in class.

Reflective Journaling

Reflective journaling helps students become more aware of their strengths and areas for growth as learners so that they can develop more effective strategies. It can be especially helpful when it's done immediately after learning to process what did and didn't work, where the learner was successful or got stuck, and what problem-solving strategies they employed in the moment.

Reflective journals can take the form of a notebook that is devoted to this type of writing or handouts provided during the lesson. Journal entries should focus on students' learning experiences, reflecting on what they have learned, what they found challenging, and how they might approach similar tasks in the future. While students may ask to be able to type their thoughts on a computer, there can be benefits to doodling, sketching, listing, or writing out thoughts by hand. If technology must be used, a digital pen and a resource such as Notability (https://notability.com) bridge the gap between paper and pen and an electronic device.

Using Scaffolds

Teachers can use scaffolds, even in online environments, to facilitate metacognitive reflection. Hagan and colleagues (2020) share the RECAP framework to support students' learning and metacognitive reflection:

- **Reflect** on your week
- **Explain** what you learned
- **Compare** your work
- **Act** on feedback
- **Plan** for success (p. 41)

The authors state, "The weekly RECAP structure is effective because it not only encourages students to engage with the course at the start of each week but fosters self-reflection and self-regulated learning" (p. 60). The advantage of using a scaffold like this is that it incorporates training in how to apply reflective practices as part of students' learning.

Employing Concept Maps

Concept maps are visual tools that illustrate cognitive connections. These maps allow learners to see relationships among ideas, concepts, or terms and are another tool to facilitate metacognitive reflection. Critically, the process of creating a concept map often reveals gaps or misunderstandings the student has, which can prompt them to seek out additional learning to fill in those gaps.

According to Ritchhart and colleagues (2009), concept maps in grades 3 through 11 "are indeed rich vehicles for uncovering students' conceptions of thinking in a way that is accessible both to teachers and students" (p. 156). The researchers saw growth in students' metacognitive thinking across the duration of their study of concept map use. More important, they saw an increase in how much students value thinking about their thinking, which indicates that making reflective metacognition valued in the classroom creates a climate that fosters reflection by students as a natural part of the learning process (Ritchhart et al., 2009).

Notice how Figure 3.3's concept map example captures evidence of this student's extensive understanding of graphs—not just what graphs are and how they are categorized but also when to use them. Being able to articulate these relationships is a vital component of this subject matter.

Co-Created Rubrics

Another opportunity for students to be metacognitive in their learning was introduced in Nancie Atwell's (1998) text, *In the Middle: New Understandings About Writing, Reading, and Learning*. Atwell describes setting grading rubrics with students by reviewing samples of student work and discussing what they notice about the quality and essential elements of the assignment. Engaging in this type of metacognitive work is powerful for students. They take ownership of their learning and the expectations set as they see what the teacher sees, register the characteristics of effective work, and determine grading criteria collaboratively. Even though the teacher guides the discussion, students engage more deeply through metacognitive reflection.

Figure 3.3
Example: Student Concept Map About Graphs

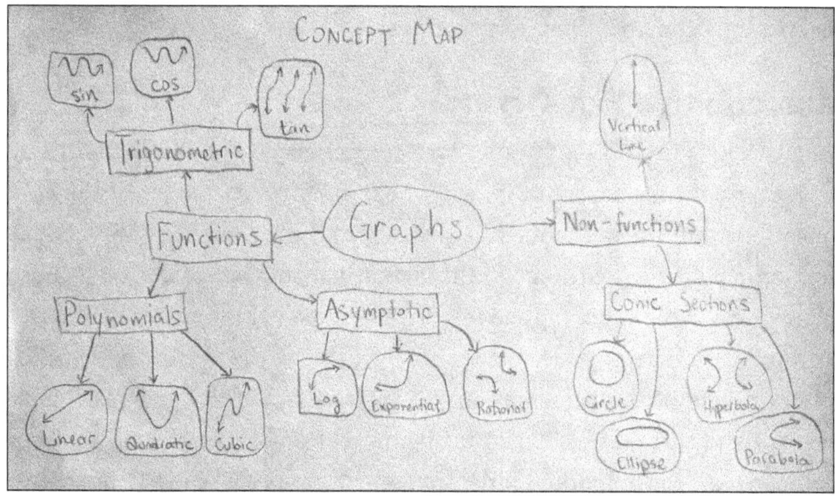

Think-Ink-Pair-Share

The Think-Ink-Pair-Share strategy supports students' metacognitive reflection by having them formulate their own thoughts and then compare them with others. It starts with giving students explicit time to think about the topic, their reactions, and their questions. The second step is for students to write down those thoughts in lists, sentences, or even graphic organizers and sketches. This solidifies their thinking and prepares them for the sharing stage. Next, they pair up with classmates and share their reflections with one another. Students should have time to both talk and listen to their partner. This time can be made more meaningful by having students follow up by sharing back one thing they noticed about the partner's thoughts: a connection, a question, or an elaboration. If students are sharing opinions, they can even identify which piece of evidence from their partner was the most effective argument and why. They may also create a synthesis of the pair's most important points, collectively.

At times, you may want to add a "square" step, in which students "square their thinking" by joining a second pair of students to add depth to the conversation (Himmele & Himmele, 2017). Again, students should be reminded to listen to their classmates, not just share. Finally, the class engages in a whole-group discussion.

By the end of the process, students can better understand and articulate their own thoughts, leaving them better prepared to share these thoughts with peers to confirm, further develop, or even adjust their thinking in light of additional information and other perspectives.

Metacognitive Exit Tickets

Exit tickets are still a popular way to end class, especially following the introduction of new content. Instead of asking for a summary of the content or questions that the students still have about the learning, invite students to reflect on what they learned, identify what learning strategies or techniques worked best for them during the lesson, and make a plan to act on that learning. Using exit tickets to metacognitively debrief the lesson both solidifies the importance of the information in the student's mind and pinpoints key successes and difficulties. Consider using technology platforms that enable anonymous and/or individual reflection so that you don't have to hand out and collect papers. You can then revisit the previous day's reflections with students as an activator to the next day's learning to confirm understandings, clear up confusion, and help students reconnect with previous successes (either strategic or content-based).

Post-Assessment Reflection

Students can also use metacognitive strategies to evaluate their test preparedness and understand post-assessment results, shifting agency and responsibility for outcomes to students in a tangible way. One 7th grade teacher, in a school district that offered retests to allow students to focus on learning content and skills instead of their performance on one-time, high-stakes assessments, built metacognitive reflection into the retesting procedure. Before retaking the assessment, the student needed to share, in writing, how they had prepared for the original assessment, how they felt going into the assessment, what surprised them about the outcome, and why they thought they were surprised. This level of analysis puts the onus of preparation on students, giving them control of their learning and the outcome.

Using these reflection data, the teacher would respond to a student who wrote, "I didn't understand the material," with learner-initiated strategies they could use to address the issue in the future, such as sharing their confusion with the teacher to trigger a reteaching session or attending homework club to engage in tutoring. Most often, this type of metacognitive reflection led students to recognize their role in preparing for assessments and become more engaged and proactive.

Final Thoughts on Reflection as a Mirror

One question we always get is how to overcome students' reluctance or resistance to being asked to reflect. Just as with any skill, metacognitive reflection takes practice and time; lots of us—and lots of students—can relate to the reluctance to put in the work. And reflection is not the only area facing that challenge; with writing skills, for example, after years of minimal writing, and/or writing to prompts only, students often groan when we ask them to write. But over time, with modeling, encouragement, and practice, they can regain their joy for writing. We must be patient with students who are used to adults telling them what to think, how to think, when to think, and so on. There never seems to be enough time in school to let things percolate or to allow students to grapple with something for more than a minute or two before we have to move on to another class or lesson.

With repeated, low-stakes exposure to metacognitive reflection practices, especially those that don't require formal writing (e.g., reflecting with jottings, sketchnotes, or turn-and-talk opportunities), students will grow to appreciate reflection and become more proficient in it. Like all things we want students to internalize, we first must model metacognitive reflection, scaffold it, and provide explicit opportunities for skill development. After time and practice, students will be ready to reflect on their own as a natural part of their learning process.

The most important reason to build in time for metacognitive reflection is to help make students' learning more meaningful, more memorable, and *theirs*. So often, in hopes of covering the year's curriculum in a limited time, we skip the vital steps of allowing students to examine and process their thinking, and we wind up reteaching the material. If we allow students the gift of metacognitive reflection, their learning will be more solid. They will understand the active role they play in learning: how they learn and why knowing that is relevant and important to them. In the end, building in time for metacognitive reflection saves time because learning "sticks" and repeated lessons/directions/conversations are required less often. Additionally, it gives students agency over themselves as learners as they explore what strategies work and what they need to adjust. It puts the job of learning squarely on the students' shoulders, making them partners in the learning process, not just witnesses to the presentation of information.

Students Share

In this video, middle and upper division students from The Janus School in Mount Joy, Pennsylvania, talk about their reflective practices.

Questions for Individual Reflection

1. How often do you make time to think about your thinking so that you can share your personal metacognitive experiences with your students as a model?
2. How has metacognitive reflection supported a supervision conversation you've had in the past?
3. How can reflecting on your thinking help you better communicate your teaching expertise to a newer colleague or student teacher?

Questions to Discuss with Colleagues

1. Where do you see a lack of metacognitive reflection impeding student learning?
2. Where could you build metacognitive reflection naturally into your curriculum to better solidify students' learning?
3. How do you see metacognition engaging your students to be more active learners?

4

Reflection as a Map: Metastrategic Thinking and Goal Setting

Hitch your wagon to a star.
—Ralph Waldo Emerson

When planning for this chapter on reflection as a map, Lynne journaled about how she tracked her progress toward her goals, such as earning a reading specialist certificate and, later, a doctoral degree in educational leadership. But the goals she thought about weren't just professional ones. A personal journey to prepare for a trip to Italy with her husband provided the perfect metaphor for using reflection as a map.

Lynne struggles with tendinitis, and with two months to go before leaving on the trip, she realized her customary exercise routine of laps around the local mall in ballerina-type flats was creating a huge problem. With shooting pains in the back of her heels, ankles, and calves, she visited an orthopedic doctor who diagnosed her after asking her to walk across the office on tiptoes—something she could not even begin to do. He wrote a script for six weeks of physical therapy (PT), and she despaired of making the trip to Italy, which would comprise a lot of walking, sometimes on cobblestones and staircases with no banister to hold onto for support.

She began a daily routine of exercises prescribed by the physical therapist and faithfully kept her PT appointments. She started wearing sneakers around the house, then added walks in the yard, and finally moved on to short strolls in the neighborhood. Three times a week she walked on a rubberized track to minimize the impact on her feet. Along the way she kept a journal about not just her physical progress but also about the places she would visit in Rome, Florence, and Venice, inspired by travel guides and pictures on the internet. She set three important goals to prepare for her trip—be able to walk at least two miles each day, stand in one place for 10 to 15 minutes, and walk up and down a set of stairs without holding onto a railing. To that end, she started using a standing desk for computer work and practiced the stairs at home.

It took a long time, but Lynne saw definite progress, and her dream of vacationing in Italy was once again within reach. She started by evaluating where she was, setting goals with the aid of her physical therapist and doctor. As she worked toward her objectives, she noted the changes in her physical and mental state and used that information to adjust her plans so that she would continue to improve. The ongoing feedback from her own body changing and growing stronger gave her further reasons to make the effort.

Goal setting is powerful. People who set goals achieve more in school, at work, and in life. Goals sharpen our focus, helping us target our energy into specific outcomes, channel our work, and enhance our effectiveness.

Can you think of a time when you tracked your progress toward an important goal? What data did you gather, and how did you keep track of your progress? What did your journey toward a goal teach you about yourself? What did you learn about the value of reflection? How can you connect what you learned with how you approach goal setting with your students?

What Do We Mean by *Metastrategic Reflection*?

Lynne's reflection process involved intentionally thinking about what her end goal was (Italy) and how she would get there (through dedicated exercise and monitoring her progress)—in other words, metastrategic thinking. Rather than looking back on what was learned (reflection as a mirror) or analyzing the learning and how it was achieved (reflection as a magnifying glass), metastrategic reflection (reflection as a map) looks *forward,* making constant adjustments in response to self-regulation.

Metastrategic reflection is the process of thinking about where you've been—about evaluating an experience you've had so that you can look ahead with more self-awareness. It involves starting with an end goal and then mapping a strategic plan to reach it. It might also involve being able to predict the effects of actions or concepts and determine what the most likely outcome will be. The practice of metastrategic reflection is especially important in developing effective persuasion and argumentation, because it gives learners the information they need to predict counterpoints to their claims and plan responses.

Students who engage in metastrategic reflection learn to recognize their strengths and weaknesses in learning, problem solving, and decision making by thinking about what they want to know and how they plan to know it. Metastrategic reflection helps students develop more effective strategies, monitor their progress, identify challenges, and adjust their approach to reaching their goals accordingly. Along the way, they gain a deeper understanding of their cognitive processes, leading to even better goal setting and self-assessment.

Reflection as a Map: Metastrategic Thinking

Metastrategic reflection requires a growth mindset—a belief in the capacity to adapt and change. Students with a growth mindset are resilient and persevere despite difficulty. They are the confident ones who are open to trying out new ideas and strategies and don't let setbacks get them off track (Yeager & Dweck, 2012). Conversely, students with a fixed mindset—such as those who have been conditioned to believe that they will "never get it" because of patterns of repeated failure in their personal life, academic life, or both—don't want to risk more failure or negative reactions from teachers or peers, so they stop trying. The negativity grows deeper, and the learning gap gets wider.

In any scenario, teaching students about mindset and the choices they make, the attitudes they possess, and the belief system they subscribe to is essential. There's far more to teaching students about goal setting than saying, "OK, class! Let's set a goal." For most of us, students included, goal setting is encumbered by deep, personal emotions that have formed over the years and put limits on what we think is possible. No matter where a student is when it comes to growth mindset, it's up to us, their teachers, to put the tools in their hands and hearts that will help them make reflection an everyday habit—one that can truly change their lives for the better.

Why a Map?

Maps have been an essential tool for humans throughout history. From ancient civilizations to modern times, mapmaking has played a crucial role in helping us navigate, understand, and interpret the world around us. There are myriad benefits to mapmaking that extend far beyond simple navigation. A map offers a tangible way to create a visual representation of space that enhances our understanding of a layout and makes relationships between different geographic features clear. There are many kinds of maps—climate, political, weather, population, physical, resource, and so on—but they all help us develop a better understanding of our surroundings. Studying maps helps us comprehend the scale, distances, and relative positions of various locations.

Another benefit to mapmaking is its contribution to navigation and way finding. Maps provide detailed information about roads, landmarks, and geographical features to help us reach our destinations efficiently. Whether you're planning to travel to a foreign country or mapping out a cross-country route to travel in your RV to national parks across the United States, maps guide you to your desired destination and keep you on the right path. They are also indispensable tools for planning and decision making across a wide range of contexts, such as city planning or identifying vulnerable areas to inform disaster evacuation plans.

The reflection-as-a-map metaphor makes a great deal of sense in this context of encouraging student agency and forward thinking (see Figure 4.1). As we reflect on our journey to reach a given destination, we learn how to adapt quickly to shifts in expectations and the value of perseverance through all the hard stuff. We can make informed decisions. In a nutshell, maps guide us to explore our inner landscapes and understand our journey toward our goals, similar to how we use maps to navigate physical terrain.

Figure 4.1

Reflection as a Map: Metastrategic Thinking

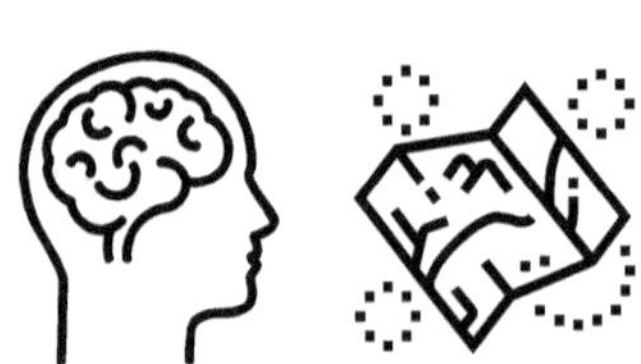

This facet of reflection focuses on providing students with opportunities to plan and problem-solve prior to starting an assignment or while working on it. It asks students to think, plan ahead, and predict what unexpected variables might affect the outcome of their project, experiment, or assignment.

Multilingual Learners: Planning for Success

Reflection as a map (metastrategic thinking) provides opportunities for multilingual learners to plan for success regardless of challenges related to language. Planning ahead and planning new ways to deal with expected and unexpected obstacles is not usually reliant on language, so being a metastrategic thinker allows MLs to demonstrate their problem-solving skills. It can also help them plan for times when they know language will be challenging. Thinking metastrategically can help students understand what works for them and how to employ strategies that will help them with their present task. Just as awareness of metacognition in the role of learning can empower MLs and lay the groundwork for success, metastrategic awareness can help them deliberately plan for that success, encompassing skills that will far outlast the lesson being taught.

Whoever is doing the majority of the reading, writing, sharing, planning, and talking is doing the majority of the learning; too often, this person is the teacher rather than the students. Learning floats on a sea of talk (Britton, 1970); in other words, when students articulate their learning, they strengthen their understandings as well as support their peers in developing their own articulation of understandings. There is power in the classroom community operating as a giant think tank, where students are asked to pause, think, consider, and help one another process their learning. Conversely, when teachers own the talk, students can passively forgo their own processing, limiting their opportunities to make sense of the material. Using talk to create understanding, rather than to assess it, enhances the ability to apply learning in new situations and encourages higher-order thinking. Discourse (academic conversation in pursuit of learning) allows students to hear and reflect on the power of their ideas as well as deepen their understanding of others' thinking.

Reflection as a map involves visualizing both the journey and the destination and strategizing about connecting the two. Reflection can and should happen at any time, but it's important to first set aside daily time for it. Teachers need to invite learners to share their work, their thinking, their goals, and their journey. Reflection as a map also requires students to meet with teachers and peers and hold self-conferences along the way to seek specific feedback on their work toward short- and long-term goals. Students need to ask themselves (and others) questions that encourage a close examination of their performance during a recent lesson or unit and evaluation relative to the goals they've set. Then they can move forward and establish new goals.

When students take time to consider what they have learned and how they have grown, learning lasts longer and is much more impactful. Reflection helps the brain recall and make connections with prior learning, leading learners to integrate and contextualize their experiences, commit them to long-term memory, and reapply or transfer what they've learned in new ways—the universal goal of education. Intentionally using reflection to establish goals sets the stage for systematically working through their understandings as they engage in distinct thinking processes shaped by their habits of mind and academic strengths. Their next steps are to find new opportunities to learn, bolstered by growth in ownership, agency, and knowledge of themselves as learners.

Many students are visual learners and thus benefit from using a chart to track their goals and the path to achieve them, as well as how that path changes over time as they read, experiment, discuss, confer, and reimagine the possibilities. Figure 4.2 contains a template for a chart that students can use to track their thinking. By guiding students to plan, monitor, and evaluate their learning and progress, the scaffold empowers them to become more independent and effective learners. Teachers can also display this format on an anchor chart to encourage students to use it across content areas.

Figure 4.2

Template: "Documenting My Journey" Chart

Documenting My Journey: Reflections in [*Subject Area*] Class			
My original thought(s):	**Feedback from other sources** *(peers, readings, brainstorming, videos, teacher(s), larger community, family member, self-assessment, other)*	**What I'm thinking now** *(my new and revised thinking, reassessment, amendment, modifications)*	**Goal(s)** *(short- and/or long-term goals for a new unit of study, writing assignment, research project, reflection notebook, other)*
Date:			
Date:			
Date:			

Developing a Culture of Question Makers

Students take their cues from their teachers as they learn to become question makers. The depth and interest levels in class discussions are often influenced by the kinds of questions we ask students to ponder. Asking questions with one "right" answer—comprehension on a literal level—often means the questions are too easy. We want students to dig deeper for meaningful discussions in partnerships and small- and whole-group gatherings and articulate their thoughts in writing to reflect on their perspective, others' perspectives, and possible revisions to their thinking. Therefore, it is important for educators to model what good questions look like, sound like, and feel like. Try asking yourself some simple questions about your questions:

- Is the question open-ended or closed—in other words, can students imagine the possibilities or is there only one right answer?
- Does the question rely too heavily on background knowledge students do not possess?
- Is the question too easy, too vague, or too narrow?
- Does the question ask students to connect their learning with their lives outside the school day?
- Does the question relate to an important problem?
- Is the question asking students to apply what they've learned?

Journal prompts are a different form of questioning that guides students on their reflection journey. Some students' written responses will lead to asking new questions and responding to them; some will build on questions others have posed during lessons, discussions, and conferences. As students begin their journey toward new goals, reflection journaling (as depicted in Figure 4.3's adult-created example) helps them develop new perspectives and meanings and continue to enlarge and revise their understanding. A reflection requirement like journaling also communicates to students the importance of prolonging discussion even after reaching initial goals. Journaling can take many forms: full sentences, lists, graphic organizers, drawings or photos with labels, or even cartoons. Any of these formats can provoke reflection.

At any grade level, consider facilitating reflection as a map by providing some reflective questions and/or sentence stems to guide students to think about what they have learned over time and project where they want to go next. A posted anchor chart is a handy way to present a collection of pertinent prompts. Here are some simple ones to get students started in their reflective journals and discussions:

- *I keep wondering if/about...*
- *This idea/direction is important to me because...*
- *It's surprising that...*
- *Or maybe...*
- *What I'm really trying to say is...*
- *I wonder if...*
- *So far, I have tried...*
- *A change(s) I am thinking about is...*
- *What do I now know and understand clearly?*
- *What connections can I make to my personal knowledge?*
- *What did I learn about myself as a* [writer, reader, social scientist, mathematician, etc.]?
- *What feedback did I get from my teacher or other students that was important to me?*
- *What strengths have I noticed about myself?*
- *What are the next steps in my learning journey?*
- *What strengths and experiences can I bring to meet challenges in the unit of study we are about to begin?*

Figure 4.3

Example: Reflective Journal Entry About Energy

In the beginning: What I was thinking to get started	New ideas from reading, viewing, brainstorming, planning, conferring, experimenting, or exploring online platforms	What I am presently thinking
How can we create a series of a minimum of three collisions? A ramp is needed for gravitational energy to create a series of collisions.	The faster an object is moving, the more energy it has. When objects collide, the contact forces a transfer of energy.	A steeper, longer ramp will provide more energy for the toy car to build collision energy for a domino effect with empty cereal boxes. This process converts the energy stored in each upright cereal box to kinetic energy as it falls and impacts the next cereal box, creating a domino effect.

Classroom Snapshot: Using a Reflection Tool to Look Forward

Lynne joined Greg's 4th grade math classes to observe how he uses the Compass Protocol (see Appendix J) to introduce student reflection. After distributing copies of the protocol, Greg asked his students to think about the math unit they had just completed.

They began by rating how they felt about the unit and their efforts to complete it, then moved on to documenting what was difficult for them and what could be done to be more successful in the future. Next, they highlighted specific strengths, actions, and attitudes evidenced in their unit work. Finally, they made a plan and set goals for their work with the next unit, topping it all off by sharing their reflections with a small group of peers.

To scaffold the students' work, Greg provided an extensive checklist of big ideas they could use to help respond to the reflection questions (see Appendix K for sample Challenges and Strengths Checklists for math and other content areas). Greg also modeled reflective thinking aloud for the class. He began to see that his students might be experiencing vocabulary overload and realized he needed to be more intentional about helping them remember, understand, and mentally anchor new words as they navigated the unit. He brainstormed possibilities such as creating flash card decks and anchor charts with drawings and definitions of 2D figures. Greg also talked about self-advocacy and his process of looking over his lesson plans after he taught them—highlighting things that did not go smoothly, underlining things he could repeat, and troubleshooting with his colleague.

Greg's modeling paid off. The students were able to reflect on the unit of study using language from the "Challenges and Strengths Checklist: Math" to complete the Compass Protocol with descriptions, examples, and specific explanations. The students were eager to share their reflections and were comfortable doing so through a mathematical lens. A strong buzz in the room indicated their high level of engagement. The small-group discussions helped individual students make their thinking concrete and supported them to look forward with a new understanding of possible changes or adjustments they could make to be more successful and overcome previous barriers to learning.

Many students were eager to volunteer their thoughts by sharing with the whole group. One student talked about trying to understand her math anxiety and taking slow, deep breaths while focusing on the mantra *I can do this*. She noted that Greg's positive feedback and connections to how math is relevant to everyday life and students' interests were very helpful in lowering her stress level and helping her think about math in a positive way.

Reflection with Conferences in Elementary Classrooms

Conferring with students is a reliable way to learn about their experience with setting goals for themselves. If the concept is new to them, sharing a list of goals that they can choose from can get them started. Many teachers ask students to choose a goal, and then they select an additional goal for each student. As students become more familiar with designing goals, they will need less support.

Students can embark on goal setting as early as kindergarten. In Kolleen's classroom, kindergarten students wrote in their journals daily and had conferences with Kolleen on a regular basis to develop their writer's identity. By March, they were ready to choose a goal to work on for the next several weeks. After reading their journals carefully, Kolleen chose several doable goals to present to the class. The first goal, adding spaces between words, was appropriate for a few of her kindergartners. The second goal involved writing fluency—adding more sentences to their writing to illustrate details.

Kolleen presented three goal suggestions on a chart in front of the class:

1. I will add a space between words.
2. I will add ending punctuation.
3. I will add more details to my story.

She read each goal, explained what it meant, and then asked for student volunteers to restate the goals as they understood them. Then students decided which goal they wanted to work on. Each one rewrote their goal on a sticky note with their name on it, then brought the sticky note up to the front of the classroom and placed the note under the goal they chose. It was amazing to watch them do this. Not one student tried to look at what another classmate was writing; they were focused on what would be a good fit for *themselves.*

Later, Kolleen held conferences with small groups of students in which they elaborated on how they would work on their goals. Hannah suggested adding color words, size words, and feeling words to provide more details. James suggested that details could also be added to pictures on a journal page. He noted, "You can do this before you start to write the words or after that." Joseph shared that he was meeting his goal of adding more sentences to his entries by writing two to four sentences instead of his previous one-sentence entries.

Harper, a confident and enthusiastic writer, was ready to think about endings. Her story about her mom's interview had details, several sentences, and ending punctuation. As Harper and Kolleen reread her story together and aloud, Kolleen talked about how authors often end their stories by telling how they are feeling. She referred to *Last Stop on Market Street* by Matt de la Peña (2015) as a mentor text that had been shared in class. Subsequent to the conference, Harper added a sentence to share her excitement about the interview and used an exclamation mark to emphasize her feelings.

When you model how to write a goal that is important and doable, use language students relate to, depending on their age level, as opposed to language that comes directly from the lesson plan. This helps students take ownership of the process as they work toward setting their own goals. Use anchor charts to display goals that are appropriate for a unit of study or even long-term goals for the semester. Here are some examples of goals you might share with students:

- *I will write using clear, informational details that teach my reader about my topic.*
- *I will read for the bigger messages or themes the author is trying to share with me.*
- *I will use both my reading and math strategies to solve real-world problems.*
- *I will use different social scientist lenses (sociologist, historian, geographer, archaeologist) to build an understanding of life on the Nile in ancient Egypt.*

Don't forget to remind students that goals are targets that can be revised when necessary. They may find themselves expanding or narrowing their goals as they work toward achieving them.

A Journey, Not a One-Time Event

When we think of reflection as a map, we recognize the possibility of adjusting our route as we move toward our goals. As students learn more, their aims become more detailed and refined. Hattie's research (2009) notes the positive outcomes produced when learners use self-reflection to monitor their own progress, suggesting that self-evaluation strongly influences student achievement. These measures can involve practices such as asking questions, having conversations with others, keeping a reflection journal, responding to a rubric, or engaging in a more formal, written self-evaluation. As the ones embarking on the learning journey, students come to understand that although they won't be traveling alone, success in meeting their goals is ultimately their responsibility. This understanding then fosters students' sese of ownership and agency.

An Administrator's Angle

In this video, Stephanie Landis, Boyertown Area School District's director of curriculum and instruction, digs a little deeper into a critical piece of goal work: conversations with students that prompt them to reflect on "where they are in the process."

Supporting learner self-monitoring starts with opportunities for students to set their own learning goals, pause and reflect in their journal, respond to admit/exit slips, and engage in self-evaluation. Studies reveal that students who reflect through journaling use more cognitive strategies during a learning task. They show more sophisticated conceptions of their learning, greater awareness of cognitive strategies, and more abstract thinking (Lew & Schmidt, 2011). This is because journaling is not just about producing information; it allows students to process their learning in ways that make sense to them.

Create an anchor chart of reflection-promoting questions and sentence stems to post in a key location in the classroom. (Chapter 5 goes into anchor charts in more depth.) Students can use these prompts for journaling or as admit/exit slips. One effective application for exit slips is to use them as admit slips the next day to bring students right back to the previous class session. Sharing responses with a partner or small group can stimulate critical thinking and act as a springboard to link new learning with existing schema. In addition, a quick review of student responses informally assesses understanding of new or old concepts and helps determine who needs additional clarification or assistance from the teacher. Perhaps the biggest benefit comes from hearing their classmates' reflections, which can lead students to further revise their own reflections and goals, or spark the courage to ask questions or let their teacher know they are confused.

A Teacher's Take

In this video, Beverly DeRise, an instructor and professional development and research associate at The Janus School, talks about using prompts to ignite the working memory that's key to reflection, to power discourse, and to solicit evidence of understanding.

Here are some examples of journaling or admit/exit slip prompts:

- *List what you still need to learn to reach your goal.*
- *What strengths and knowledge do you already have that will help you reach your goal?*
- *How do you plan on using your strengths, knowledge, or process when you tackle new learning in the next unit or another content area, or when you set a new learning goal?*
- *What do you imagine having to do first to reach your goal? After that?*
- *Who can help you reach this goal? Specifically, what will you need from them?*

Students should revisit the goals they have set for themselves as often as possible. Before and immediately after students are engaging with the lesson are good times for this step, bookending daily learning experiences with reflection. Ask students to review their goals and plans and set intentions for their work. Students can share their goals and reflective journal entries in individual or group conferences with the teacher. Here are a few ideas for prompts that can help students build intentions:

- *What can I do today that will help me work toward my goal?*
- *What's puzzling or tangled up in my thinking?*
- *What feedback do I need as I work toward my goal?*
- *As I study the plan, what adjustments can I make to customize it with all I have learned and done so far?*
- *What are my intentions for the work I will accomplish today? Tomorrow?*
- *Where did I get stuck due to a gap in my understanding? How can I go back and find what I need?*
- *What is important to remember about what I did here?*
- *What do I need to do to persevere?*

- *How will I know when I have succeeded?*
- *How am I working toward my goal? What can I do differently?*
- *If I have more time, what could I choose to investigate further?*
- *How am I different because of my journey?*

This reflection work can be done individually, with a partner, or in small groups. It can take just three to five minutes or last longer under certain conditions (e.g., mid-unit reflection to adjust goals). But it is imperative to maintain a fluid interaction between reflection and goals throughout a unit.

Setting goals identifies a clear pathway to success, allowing students to focus on what they need to do. This goes a long way toward preventing students from becoming overwhelmed, frustrated, or discouraged. It lessens feelings of being disheartened and encourages learners to spend time on activities that contribute to their goals. Goal setting boosts students' confidence. When they make progress toward achieving their goals, they gain self-esteem and develop identities as readers, writers, thinkers, mathematicians, artists, and so on. Confidence in their abilities is important to their self-image in the long run and will help them tackle future goals with less anxiety. With newfound confidence, they can continue to set more difficult and far-reaching goals.

There are myriad ways to gather data to evaluate students' reflective journaling practices. Checklists, audio and video files, questionnaires, and observations during conferences can all provide important information. Teachers can also develop a simple rubric to evaluate students' skills in creating reflective journal entries and use the information gathered to give feedback to help them develop those skills. See Figure 4.4 for an example.

Reflection and Research

Teaching students how to become real researchers is often difficult, as many have already settled into a habit of downloading primary and secondary sources, copying from them verbatim, and piecing the acquired information into a "research paper" of sorts. Guiding upper elementary and even middle school students away from plagiarism, misunderstandings, and misrepresentation can be a challenge. Guiding learners to reflect and set goals for themselves promotes "buy-in," keeps them engaged in the experience, and helps maintain attention on the purpose and value of their efforts and actions (Willis & Willis, 2020).

Figure 4.4

Example: Rubric for a Reflective Journal, Grades K–8

Rubric: Reflective Thinking		
I've arrived! Well-developed thinking	**Almost there!** Developing and showing effort/growth	**Not there yet; keep trying!** Working toward proficiency
Learner reflects daily. Entries show high level of reflection with consideration for other points of view, well-developed ideas, documentation of progress toward goal, support/ confirmation of original ideas/plan and revision based on new learning along the journey.	Learner reflects frequently. Entries show some evidence of reflective thought such as consideration for other points of view, revision based on new learning, or confirmation of original ideas, but not all these facets are present and developed.	Entries are sparse and occasional. Learner's journal entries are short, generic, and not developed to show changes in thinking as new learning is acquired.

It is valuable to teach students how to set small goals along the way. In Lynne's 5th grade class, students stop at the end of each research period to create an entry in their journal about what they learned or accomplished that day. They also develop their research ideas by pulling from a minimum of three sources and filling a note card with information from memory (practicing how to paraphrase) and devising questions generated by this information (practicing reflection). In the beginning of the project, Lynne models this practice to provide students with scaffolding support.

The questions guide students forward on their research path. Students use one-sentence summaries of their day's learning to write a short-term goal for the next class period. They also use their journals to record questions and ideas they consider worthy of further investigation. During a final class reflection period, students discuss/share their notes and questions or what they hope to accomplish during the next class session. Whole-class discussions and individual or small-group conferences help students frame their research question, consider various resources, and decide their first and subsequent steps on their research journey. Lynne frequently asks students to provide a written self-evaluation at the end of the project that includes a discussion of their goals and how they fared in meeting them.

Classroom Snapshot: A Reflection Road Map for Science

What could be more satisfying to a student than being tasked with turning common materials into a chain reaction of collisions to perform a simple task? To showcase their learning about energy, a group of students used ingenuity to design chain reactions using cereal boxes, toy cars, and string.

Intrigued by how the lesson would be enhanced by student reflection, Catherine met with five students for three half-hour sessions before the activity to take them through some preparatory discussion and protocols:

- Concept and vocabulary review
- Higher-order thinking discussion
- The Looking Back to Look Ahead Protocol (see Appendix L)
- The Reflection Road Map Protocol (see Appendix M)

Catherine's small group of students began by using the Looking Back to Look Ahead Protocol to revisit what they had learned in the science unit (see Figure 4.5). Diego easily recalled key concepts as well as what surprised him and what worked during the unit. However, when he answered the question *How can I use what I learned in real life?,* his response revealed a somewhat limited view. Later, when Noah shared his response to the same question—that he could build a ramp out of scrap plywood to get something heavy up the steps at their house—it inspired Diego to imagine a real-life connection beyond applying his learning to the next activity. The group also filled out the graphic organizer on the Reflection Road Map in advance of the engineering activity (see Figure 4.6).

The room was filled with excitement and enthusiasm as students actively planned their approaches and gathered supplies. Lynne joined for the final activity. She was eager to watch students bring their designs to life and curious to see if the reflection group's project would apply their thinking in distinctive or meaningful ways. As the activity progressed, it was clear that *all* the groups demonstrated success, but distinctions emerged for the small group:

- Students spent more time collaboratively discussing design possibilities and end goals before they began construction.
- They took more frequent pauses to think and plan before they acted.
- The group celebrated moments of team success.
- They engaged in thoughtful problem-solving discussions when challenges arose.

After the activity was completed, Lynne and Catherine followed up with the group to review the experience. Lynne helped students evaluate the chain reaction they had designed, counting the number of reactions and using scientific vocabulary. Then, as she guided the group through the reflection questions from the Reflection Road Map, they collaboratively identified the three questions that resonated most by marking them with a star. Finally, each student reflected in writing on the experience (see Jada's response in Figure 4.7).

Figure 4.5

Example: Diego's "Looking Back to Look Ahead" Notes

Looking Back to Look Ahead

1. List 3 of the most important concepts, ideas, or strategies you learned: Energy and Stored Energy
   a. Energy can be Stored when Something gets lifted up
   b. Things go faster when they have more energy
   c.
2. What surprised you?
   Energy can't be Stored correctly and it doesn't work sometimes.
3. What puzzled or frustrated you?
   Something that puzzled me is how Something didn't work
4. When you encountered a problem, how did you solve it?
   I encountered a lot of problems and I solved them by ajusting the setup
5. Did you work well with classmates during group activities? What went well? What could you do differently?
   Yes I Worked well with my classmate What I could of done differently was think what to do first then do it instead of starting right away
6. How can I use what I learned in real life?
   I can use it by doing what I learned it the next activity

Authors' note: This question sheet is an adapted version of the protocol in Appendix L. Teachers can adapt all protocols to meet the needs of their individual students and communities. Flexibility is key!

Figure 4.6

Example: Graphic Organizer from Jada's Reflection Roadmap

Reflection Roadmap

The *Reflection Roadmap* helps you reflect on what you learned, how you learned it, and how you'll plan your final project. Each stop on the map has a question to guide your thinking. It's like a journey through your brain! Follow the arrows from one shape to the next to help you reflect on how you wish your journey to go.

You are the explorer! Your thoughts, ideas, sketches, and plans will lead you to the treasure of discovery and success!

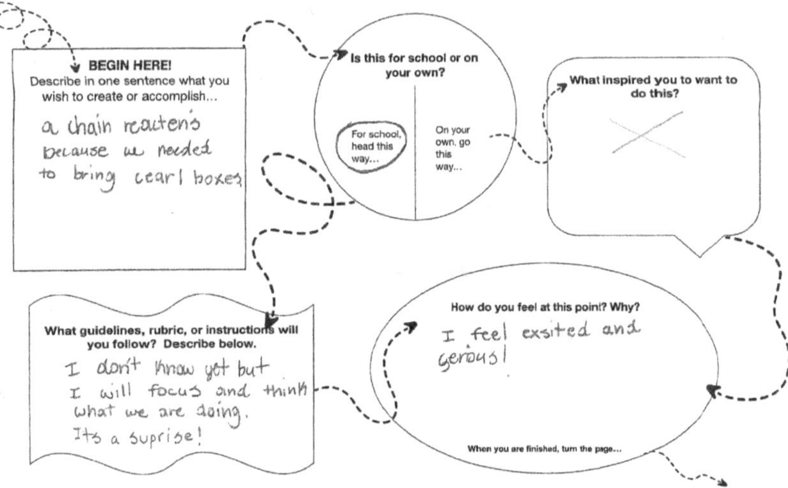

BEGIN HERE!
Describe in one sentence what you wish to create or accomplish...

a chain reacten's because we needed to bring cearl boxes

Is this for school or on your own?

For school, head this way...

On your own, go this way...

What inspired you to want to do this?

What guidelines, rubric, or instructions will you follow? Describe below.

I don't know yet but I will focus and think what we are doing. Its a suprise!

How do you feel at this point? Why?

I feel exsited and gerous!

When you are finished, turn the page...

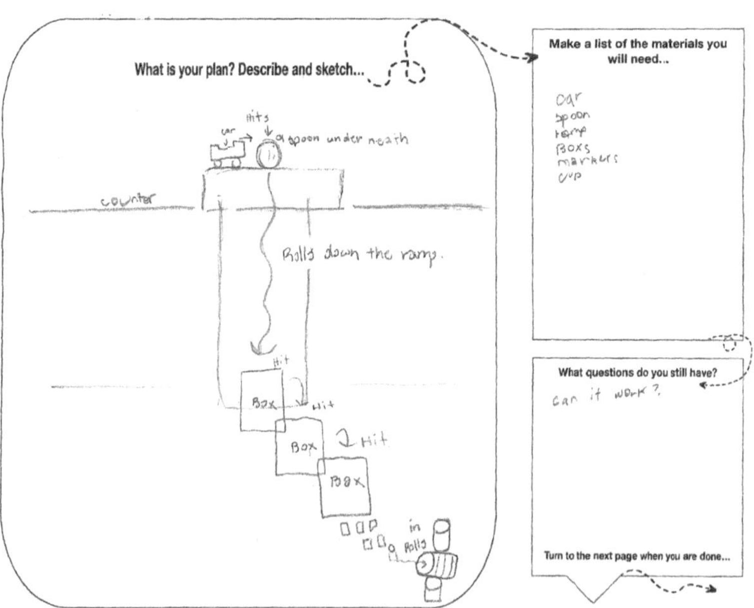

What is your plan? Describe and sketch...

Make a list of the materials you will need...

car
spoon
ramp
Boxs
markers
cup

What questions do you still have?

Can it work?

Turn to the next page when you are done...

Figure 4.7

Example: Jada's Responses to the Reflection Roadmap Questions

Like any journey, it's wise to pause along the way to reflect and ask yourself the important questions...

Look back on Learning...	What did I discover that can shed light on this project? What was tricky for me when I was learning? How did I work through it?
Stay Focused...	How can I visualize the end product? How will I adapt when something unexpected comes up? What can I do to persevere?
Problem Solve...	What is puzzling me? What caused the problem? How can I retrace my steps? Who can I collaborate with to come up with a solution?
Evaluate and Reflect	What worked? What did not work? What surprised me? What would I do differently next time? How did I grow or change as a learner during this time?

A place to reflect and park your thoughts:

what worked was the markers set up like bowling pins and one marker at the end had marble on top and rolled down in the cup. What didn't work was we put the text book like a domino but they didn't stay up and they were too hevy.

When asked in a closing discussion what they would change about this experience, Amelia volunteered, "What we should change is to make sure to try out everyone's ideas because someone else may think of something really great that works!" Students nodded their heads in agreement, and Lynne and Catherine were pleased to note the effects of the powerful learning experience.

Using Portfolios for Goal Setting

Wolf and Siu-Runyan (1996) define portfolios as "a selective collection of student work and records for progress gathered across diverse contexts over time, framed by reflection and enriched through collaboration, that has as its aim the advancement of student learning" (p. 31). Portfolios are powerful tools for students to document their growth, celebrate their learning journey, and take ownership of their education. Using visual or written summaries to explicitly connect early artifacts with more recent ones, portfolio assessment can highlight how the student's work and understanding have evolved and where it's heading.

Best of all, students are responsible for tracking and articulating how their skills, knowledge, and learning dispositions evolve. This process not only reinforces academic growth but also develops essential skills like self-assessment, goal setting, and persistence. Students learn to ask the right questions of themselves and critically analyze their work so that they can select appropriate goals for the next unit, semester, or year.

As students review their portfolios, they gain a deeper understanding of their learning process. They learn to identify what strategies work best for them and how feedback has influenced their improvements, empowering them to meet new challenges and set new goals. This kind of reflection fosters a growth mindset, encouraging students to turn challenges into opportunities for development. Appendix N contains two evaluation forms that walk students through a reflective review of their portfolios. Completing these forms synthesizes the learner's journey, celebrates their achievements, and identifies areas for continued growth.

Sharing portfolios with teachers, peers, or family members allows students to articulate their learning in meaningful ways, further solidifying their growth, helping students see a new direction forward. Portfolios are so much more than a collection of work; they are dynamic narratives of progress that inspire students to become responsible risk takers, embrace their potential, and reach for the stars.

Final Thoughts on Reflection as a Map

Anticipating a positive outcome can strengthen neural pathways in the brain associated with optimism and trigger the release of dopamine, a "feel-good" hormone. There is evidence to suggest that the dopamine-related motivation activated by optimism may also correlate to positive expectations for setting goals and wanting to achieve them (Willis & Willis, 2020). It is safe to say that overall student performance improves with goal setting. Thinking of reflection as a map helps students visualize success as they take small steps toward their end goal.

When educators understand how learning can be enriched by reflection as a map, why it is important, and how to incorporate goal setting and reflection into the journey we take to reach our goals, all students can benefit. When students are given the time and guidance to reflect along their path, they become empowered and more engaged in every activity—reading, writing, speaking, and listening. The purposeful integration of reflection to set and reach goals provides an opportunity for worthwhile change and long-lasting learning. Supporting our learners at every grade level to monitor their own progress through myriad opportunities for reflection and goal setting is a pathway to student agency and a deeper understanding of their needs and wants. Students commit to setting goals, monitoring progress, and reflecting along the way to new learning; our charge is to build in reflection time frequently until it becomes the norm.

A Teacher's Take

The effects of using reflection as a map often come quickly. Here, Greg Moll talks about some of the unexpected benefits that he's seen so far and why it's enough to put him on "Team Reflection."

Questions for Individual Reflection

1. How can metastrategic reflection help your most challenged students hold high expectations for themselves?
2. How can metastrategic reflection help you better communicate your goals and expectations to a principal/supervisor?
3. What lingering questions do you have about metastrategic reflection?
4. What new understandings do you have about the value of metastrategic reflection in your practice?

Questions to Discuss with Colleagues

1. Where could you apply the metaphor of reflection as a map to your work across content areas?
2. How could portfolios help your students explore their learning processes and become comfortable and competent with setting short- and long-term goals?
3. How do you see reflection as a map engaging your students to be more active learners?

5

Creating a Reflection-Ready Classroom

The best way to predict your future is to create it.

—*Source unknown*

Catherine recently purchased an air fryer. To fit the new appliance into her small kitchen, she needed to get rid of some unnecessary items and reconfigure her counter space—and she knew it wouldn't be a simple process. As she sketched a new layout, she realized that each decision had a domino effect: eliminating a second coffeemaker meant moving a utensil holder; moving the utensil holder meant relocating canisters. But she had a goal in mind, and she knew that her persistence would pay off. When she was done, she looked around with satisfaction. The new arrangement not only housed the new appliance but also made the kitchen more efficient than it had been before.

Similarly, you might be facing the task of rearranging your classroom space to make it more conducive to reflective practice. Consider the following as you make your plan: *Where do you learn best? What kinds of objects surround you? What do you need to reconfigure? What must be in place for you to devote time and effort into learning something challenging and new?* These questions apply regardless of grade level. Your goal is to create a positive classroom environment that will set your learners up for the long haul—one where they will be successful in meeting their goals and flourish.

Classroom Snapshot: Sticky Note Stretch

It's common for students reflecting on their learning to default to short, vague assessments. However, when given the time and tools to elaborate, many students can—and will—find gems buried beneath their surface thinking.

Matt, a high school freshman, and his classmates reflected on their growth at the end of the school year using the Sticky Note Stretch Protocol (see Appendix O). His responses to the four questions from the protocol appear in Figure 5.1. The answer to Question 2—*What's one challenge you faced this year, and how did you respond to it?*—caught our attention.

> **Sticky note response:** Dealing with not playing football
>
> **Elaboration:** One challenge I faced this year was receiving negativity about my decision to not play football and focus on other things. The mindset that helped me get through was being confident and not caring what everyone has to say about my decision. One way I can connect this is my decision to take a different science class and a lot of people told me it was a bad choice, but I ended up liking it and having a good time.

Curious to find out more, Catherine invited Matt to talk about his reflection. She learned he had been a successful football player since he was young but had become increasingly concerned about potential head injuries and the huge time commitment. Matt wanted to explore other interests, specifically learning to play the guitar and weightlifting. He received pushback from friends and their parents, who told him he would regret quitting.

Matt was also criticized by college-bound friends for choosing to take General Science Inquiry instead of Biology, but he felt the class was more aligned with his goal of attending trade school. He elaborated:

> Just because it wasn't as challenging as Biology doesn't mean it wasn't interesting, and it doesn't mean I didn't learn cool things. Something cool I remember was an experiment with different kinds of potato chips, weighing them before and after we burned them. We learned that matter can't be created or destroyed, it just turns into different forms. And I also really liked my teacher.

Matt's reflections opened the door to deep and meaningful communication where he felt seen and heard. When Matt took that step back to reflect, he was able to name and elaborate on the year's challenges and recall what he had learned—and doing so reinforced the self-awareness and confidence that empowered him to take risks and go against the tide.

Figure 5.1

Example: Matt's Responses to the Sticky Note Stretch Protocol

1. What did you learn about yourself this year, inside and outside the classroom?

Something that stood out to me about myself this year is how focused I can be, for example learning the guitar. I really wanted to learn how to play so I put a lot of effort and focus into reaching that goal. this connected to my focus going into math class. my goal was to end with an A. I put a lot of time into acheiving that goal.

2. What's one challenge you faced this year, and how did you respond to it?

One challenge I faced this year was receiving negativity about my decision to not play football and focus my time on other things. The mindset that helped me get through this was being confident and not caring what everyone has to say about my decision. one way I can connect this is my decision to take a different science class and people told me it was a bad choice. But I ended up really liking it and having a good time.

3. What's something you're proud of—big or small—that shows how you've grown?

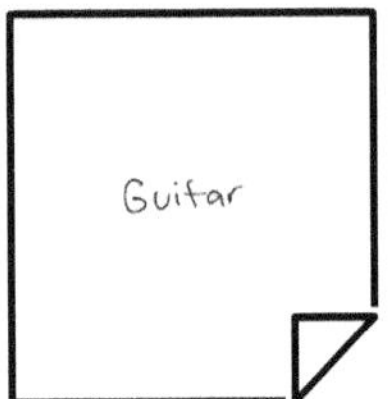

Something I am proud of is learning to play guitar. I am proud of this because it is a goal I had and I worked towards it everyday to get where I am now. This conects to how I am proud of getting an A in math because I studied every day to acheive that goal.

4. If you could give advice to your past self at the beginning of the year, what would you say?

If I could give myself advice back at the beginning of the school year I would say to not worry about what people say about you. There will always be people that have something to say and it is best to not let it consume you. this connects back to school by giving advice to just be yourself, join clubs and classes you like and don't take people's negative opinions of you.

Read over your responses: What do you notice? What stands out? Which of your responses felt surprising? Which response felt most meaningful? Why?

Supporting Emotional Safety, Respect, and Collaboration

Creating physical and emotional spaces that are conducive to reflection doesn't happen by accident. Teachers must be intentional about following a well-thought-out plan. In this chapter, we share practical tips, insights, and tools to help you create a classroom where reflection is valued and practiced on a regular basis. Developing a sense of safety that allows students to be honest and comfortable in revealing their understanding and their struggles is essential. Our goal is to create a student-centered environment where students feel safe enough to talk about their learning difficulties and successes, notice and appreciate how others solve problems, set goals, examine their thinking about their own thinking, write and revise their goals, and reflect on their progress toward those goals. Teachers can do their part by building a sense of collaboration and respect for students' strengths, including their diverse background knowledge and lived experiences.

Classroom Snapshot: Getting Past Emotional Barriers

Academic success can be especially difficult for students with emotional barriers. While these students may have a desire to learn and grow, they often lack the tools (or the ability to access tools they've been given) to move past their emotions to learn. This was true for Leia, a 4th grader who came to class most days feeling frustrated, angry, and confused. Her confusion often gave way to anger, which fueled disruptive behavior such as making loud noises, pestering others, and challenging the teacher. She would escalate quickly and shut down, thwarting her teacher's attempts to problem-solve with her. Still, it was clear that Leia was yearning to be successful. She would often be the first to enter the room and walk straight to the teacher announcing, "I'm going to have a good day today. I really am."

To give Leia what she needed and honor her desire to succeed, Catherine created the Jump-Start Reflection Protocol (see Appendix P). This 10-question tool is designed to help students identify where they are emotionally, name the barriers, and create a plan using familiar strategies. The idea is to have students reflect prior to the lesson and then reflect again afterward so they can see for themselves how the reflection process helps them overcome the barriers.

When Catherine asked Leia to meet with her at the start of class, Leia, eager for connection, was excited to spend time one-on-one. Together, they worked through each question, stopping when Leia needed examples for clarification. Leia's responses to the protocol appear in Figure 5.2.

Figure 5.2

Example: Leia's Jump-Start Reflection Responses

Take a few moments to pause, reflect, and answer the questions below to help jump-start your learning today:

1. Describe what you are learning or what task you are to complete.

   Write an essay based on a storey

2. What are you feeling? Are your feelings a roadblock to moving on?

   I cant focus on all of this
   I feel confused frstrated angry

3. What is preventing you from learning or doing the task?

   I dont understand what to write

4. When you've been in a similar situation in the past, what helped jump-start your learning?

   I go bak to the very start and I ~~restart~~ rethink my write ing. I go bak to the grafic organiser

5. What adjustments will you make to help you jump-start your learning or task today?

   take a deep brath and calm down
   I will not sarabel out the words

Stop here and try to engage in your work again. After you finish your learning or task, answer questions 6 to 10.

I feel releef

6. Describe what you learned when you returned to your learning or task.

   I figered out that if I pay atantion an go bak and reread you can figer it out

7. Were you able to complete what you needed to? If so, move on to the next question. If not, talk with your teacher.

   yes

8. Reflect on your responses to questions 1 to 5. How did going through and answering those questions help get you jump-started?

   It helps me focus on the positiv and not the negativ

9. Write an encouraging message to yourself below.

   Stay focst and worry about yourself

10. Sketch or write about what you will do next time you struggle to begin.

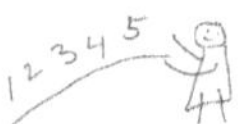

What emerged was not surprising. Leia's struggle to focus and difficulties with spelling made writing especially frustrating for her. Any kind of academic rigor was a catalyst for Leia to shut down or become angry. However, the protocol helped her acknowledge one strategy she knew but often avoided: rereading the text. Leia also identified a strategy she had been practicing outside school with her therapist: taking deep breaths. Clearly, she had a high level of self-awareness along with a repertoire of strategies, but pausing long enough to reflect on her learning was not yet second nature for her. Leia needed reflection practice and tools to make it an everyday habit.

During the lesson, Catherine made a point of reminding Leia about her desire to succeed and the strategies she could use to manage her frustration. In her post-lesson reflection, Leia expressed relief and drew a picture of herself counting to five and breathing. Leia *did* have the good day she longed for. Reflection was key in helping her manage and move past emotional barriers.

When teachers provide reflection support for students with trauma backgrounds or other types of emotional barriers, it can mean the difference between a good day and a bad one. All students need the tools and knowledge to be able to reflect on their learning, but those who come to school with emotional barriers have an especially hard time for many reasons. The Jump-Start Reflection Protocol is one way a teacher can help students move forward and experience success.

Getting to know our students is important work. Some students have struggles at home and in their community, and the safe spaces we create in our classrooms can give them a chance to feel belonging and even joy. Providing opportunities to engage in partner, small-group, and whole-class discussions helps students learn about the experiences of different readers, writers, and thinkers and gives them a chance to try out a variety of strategies and approaches to make sense of their learning and deepen their understanding of concepts.

Educators can begin the process of establishing an emotionally supportive classroom by giving students a chance to talk about what makes their classroom feel safe or unsafe to share their thinking, questions, and heartfelt reflections. It may be necessary to take time to develop discussion guidelines and protocols and teach or review social skills (e.g., how to have a successful conversation or peer conference). Routman (2018) asks us to "make sure the setting, tone, and classroom culture encourage and enhance risk-taking, deep conversations, and meaningful learning" (p. 52).

Multilingual Learners: Proactively Planning for a Positive Classroom Environment

Several years ago, Pérsida was observing a student teacher in a district with a high incidence of multilingual learners. The 3rd grade lesson was interrupted by the school secretary at the classroom door, accompanied by a new student. The student, a non-English speaker, looked terrified, which was understandable, given that she was joining a brand-new class in a brand-new country. The teacher's countenance immediately changed to a visibly angry one. She mumbled under her breath (but within earshot of the student), "I am not an ESL teacher." Pérsida's heart broke. She quickly walked over to the student and welcomed her in Spanish. Pérsida ignored the initial purpose of her visit for the remainder of her time in the classroom.

There are three main characters in this account that we'd like to address: the student, the teacher, and the student's classmates. Let's talk about the impact on each.

The Student. "Maria," who would now be in her 20s, probably still remembers the experience. Suffused with a sense of panic and feeling judged by both the teacher and her classmates, how likely is it that she was able to take advantage of opportunities to learn? The heart and mind engage in a reciprocal relationship, and we must tend to them equally well. Many MLs—especially new arrivals—are experiencing dramatic changes in their young lives. We can assume they are experiencing a type of fear that we will never know, compounded by being unable to communicate in the target language of the classroom. They need our compassion.

The Teacher. Thankfully, this is the only negative experience of its kind that Pérsida has witnessed. Most teachers are far kinder and more welcoming than the teacher she encountered. But even this extreme example reminds us of the need to check ourselves. A new student may mean more work for us, but we must be mindful of the student's need for support. Go overboard with rolling out the welcome mat. Teach your students to applaud (literally) the new student, because they are about to learn new things from someone with experiences that are different from theirs. They also will have opportunities to demonstrate kindness by assisting their new classmate in becoming proficient in English and learning, while also having opportunities to learn from the new student.

The Classmates. What type of message did this interchange send to the class? That it's acceptable to be a bully? That it's OK to overlook other people's needs because we are being "inconvenienced"? Kindness can be taught, and the classroom should be a microcosm of the world we want to live in. Provide opportunities for students to demonstrate kindness, such as creating welcome cards, checking in with one another, and introducing new students to school routines (e.g., finding the bathroom, how to order breakfast and lunch from the cafeteria, how to open a locker). Establishing clear expectations and positively reinforcing kind behavior with verbal affirmations can go a long way toward helping students understand that everyone in the classroom has deep worth, simply by virtue of existing. Every student can be a positive force in the classroom and in their world.

The Value of Daily Routines and Structures

Routman (2003) urges us to implement structures and protocols that maximize participation and learning. Instead of conducting Q&As as a quick check for understanding, we need to slow down and allow time for regular discussion across the academic day. These classroom conversations help students in many ways, such as encouraging them to imagine new pathways to solve problems and growing their unique identity as learners.

As our students become more comfortable with each other, their conversations grow in sophistication and include reflection on important ideas, concerns, and strengths as readers, writers, and thinkers. Choose places and times during class that are a natural fit for students to engage in reflection. For example, incorporate a few minutes of mindful breathing before beginning a lesson, have students reflect in a journal at the end of a lesson, or take a moment in the middle of a lesson to share things related to the content. Morning meetings can include time to reflect on what went well the day before and how students can improve today and in the future. Schedule time for sharing reflections with a partner. Teach students active listening and supportive feedback skills to foster a collaborative classroom culture.

A Teacher's Take

Maureen Vogel, an upper-level social studies teacher at The Janus School, talks about the value of "Do Nows," structured daily reflection opportunities that prompt students to think, write, and share.

Nonlinguistic representations can provide quick formative assessment data, allowing teachers to know at a glance whether students are understanding new concepts or information. Facial expressions, body language, and gestures are all examples of nonlinguistic communication. For example, students can signal their response to a new lesson with the Fist to Five technique, making a fist to show they don't understand or holding up to five fingers to represent how much they "get it." They can form a "C" with their hands when they need further clarification or communicate with a thumbs-up ("You can go on"), thumbs-down ("I don't get it"), or sideways thumb ("I sort of get it"). In her work as a literacy coach, Lynne makes it a priority to model nonlinguistic forms of communication and posts an accompanying anchor chart (like the one in Appendix Q) at the beginning of the year to serve as a visual reminder. You can make your own visuals by taking photos of your students using the signals and posting them on the chart.

Remember that gestures do not always mean the same thing across cultures. Encourage students to speak to you or write a note if a gesture makes them feel uncomfortable. For younger students, it's a good idea to introduce one or two signals each week and offer opportunities to practice using them. Nonlinguistic signals can be especially effective for MLs, students who process information more slowly, or those with other learning challenges. Nonlinguistic representations can help make the best use of instructional time while also creating a safe, positive learning environment and leveling the playing field for students who learn and think differently. When we give students structured daily opportunities to reflect on their experiences, celebrate their successes, and set goals, we empower them to become thriving lifelong learners.

Whether used as a quick check-in or a chance for slow and deliberate study, small groups give students opportunities to be heard, discuss, suggest, question, and evaluate. According to Hattie (2009), small-group instruction has a significant impact on student achievement. Small groups are a safe environment that helps students share their thinking and build their confidence and self-esteem. They provide time for peer interaction, close observation by the teacher, and opportunities to explicitly teach or reteach and check for understanding. Students can also use small groups as a platform to share reflections and practice revising their thinking in response to input from their peers.

Small-group instruction enhances the learning community by increasing peer interaction and instructional time, building students' confidence, and supporting a sharp focus on specific goals. The universal skill we want to highlight here is transfer: teaching students in small groups helps them imagine how they will infuse their new learning into their future work. Small-group settings are ideal for creating a more supportive and engaging learning environment and giving students exactly what they need at any given point in time, including support for reflective thinking.

Building Reflection into Goal-Setting Opportunities

Use reflection as a springboard for goal setting. Encourage students to set realistic and achievable goals based on their reflections and then discuss strategies for achieving them. Concluding a lesson with reflection can look like writing in a response journal, responding to one or several questions in an admit/exit slip, or completing a checklist. Giving students time to share their reflection with a partner or small group can be helpful. Sharing your thinking with others means you must think about your thinking, explain or elaborate to help others understand it, and possibly consider revising your ideas based on feedback. This type of ongoing discussion promotes inclusive spaces that cultivate student voices and help students view one another as valuable resources that can push them to learn more about themselves and their world.

Lynne and Rose Cappelli use reflection as a key component in the design of their Your Turn lessons (see Dorfman & Cappelli, 2017). For the final three to five minutes of writing workshop time, students gather to explore questions for focused revision work or share their thoughts on how they solved a problem, revised their initial draft, or tried a strategy recommended by a peer. The authors state, "Reflection, the most powerful form of revision, reaches far into the future.... Students need opportunities to help them understand what it is they can do well, and what it is that they still cannot yet do on their own" (p. 19). These understandings can lead to more targeted goal setting.

Placing one or two questions or statements on the whiteboard before reflection time and setting a timer so that students have a few minutes to think about their learning before they gather as a community is essential. Some questions might encourage students to closely examine problems that arose in their writing: *What strategy did not work for you? What strategy could you try next to solve the problem?* Others might relate directly to reflection as a map: *What goals do you have for yourself as a writer as you move into the next unit of study? Create a plan to meet your goals.*

Modeling and Anchor Charts

Teachers must build time into their day to model what reflection looks like for students. When we reflect by thinking aloud throughout our day, students learn that reflection requires hard work, plenty of concentration, and revision—as well as a willingness to consider other possibilities and understand the potential transfer of understanding that reflection affords. Share how reflection helps you reconfigure your lessons to suit your students. As we create and experiment with new ideas and approaches to our teaching, we model our thought processes for our students when we think aloud. In turn, they learn to think more imaginatively and resourcefully and adapt to new ways of thinking.

Anchor charts are a way to visibly document a learning community's thinking. They can include inspiring quotes, sentence stems to jump-start meaningful responses, reflection routines, or suggested goals. Lynne often begins the academic year with a discussion about stamina, endurance, and establishing a growth mindset supported by hard work and targeted strategies. In today's classrooms, discussion around issues of identity, lived experience, and achievable goals can promote choice and voice in the classroom while inviting students to construct meaning with their growing knowledge of their learning community.

Anchor charts are instructional tools to "anchor" students' learning. They build a culture of literacy in the classroom as teachers and students work together to record content, strategies, processes, and guidelines during minilessons and discussions that occur in small groups and the whole class. Posting anchor charts in a convenient, student-friendly location such as a bulletin board or easel in the reading center makes the community's thinking visible, permanent, and accessible to students, reminding them of what they have discovered and enabling them to incorporate new knowledge into prior knowledge. Students can refer to anchor charts during independent work as well as lesson experiences that extend a concept or skill use. They can be used to help students respond to questions about their reading, expand ideas, compose a piece of writing, contribute to discussions and problem-solving activities, or reflect in their journals.

Anchor charts can easily be stored and saved for future use. Lynne advises teachers to date their charts and give each one a working title. The anchor charts that are visible in the classroom should be the ones that students can make use of right away. The most current anchor chart can remain on a chart stand in the area where students gather for instruction and be posted on the class website or a page on the school's learning management system. Anchor charts are academic support, especially for visual learners. Key anchor charts that are used all year can adorn cabinets, closet doors, or window shades or hang on a clothesline. Some anchor charts may only be displayed during certain units of study.

Finding a management system that works is important. Anchor charts can be messy, and sometimes it's important to redo them so they are neat, organized, and easy to read. Encourage students to contribute to the anchor chart, perhaps placing their initials next to an idea they contributed. Cris Tovani (2011), in her book *So What Do They Really Know?*, says that she records student thinking identified by name so that "others in the class can see that they're not the only ones who wonder what's going on" (p. 81) and dates and saves anchor charts to serve as tangible artifacts of learning. It is not always necessary to document the individual thinking in this way, but doing it some of the time helps students feel important as they contribute to the learning community and grow as writers.

For purposes of reflection, anchor charts might contain protocols, sentence stems, or questions to prompt students to think about their thinking; develop plans and set goals; explore their identity as readers, writers, and learners; or review discourse-specific knowledge. Appendix R contains question sets for each of the facets of reflection we discuss in this book: reflection as magnifying glass, reflection as a mirror, and reflection as a map.

Our Purpose and End Goal

By examining how we delegate student responsibility for self-assessment and ongoing reflection, we can determine what is working for our students and for us, what new strategies we may choose to adapt, and what value our students place on reflection as a part of the learning process. If our goal is to teach our students *how* to learn instead of *what* to learn, we must recognize that students cannot carve out their own pathways without regularly engaging in self-reflection. When students reflect for purposes of self-assessment, goal setting, and reflection, they can make choices about what to keep and what to change. We must help our students learn to value reflection as an essential, everyday part of their learning process. Self-assessment practices are an effective way to improve student learning.

Creating a Culture of Question Makers

When we promote question makers in our classroom, we encourage students to think outside the box and develop multiple ways to respond to a problem or situation. Question makers place a high value on critical thinking and intellectual curiosity. Even when someone puts forward a controversial opinion, question makers explore the issue to reach a deeper understanding before deciding to accept or reject it. Students can learn and gain new knowledge from others who may have different approaches to thinking about things when they use their voice to ask lots of questions. Fostering a culture of question makers can make a difference in students' lives.

Remember that when we create a safe space for diverse opinions and ways of thinking, our learning community needs to be accepting, flexible, and tolerant of new ideas. Making space and time for contemplation and reflection, considering perspectives different than our own, questioning, and even just waiting for answers give us the chance to weigh in and imagine the possibilities. When we understand our students' perceptions of their learning environment, we can address factors that affect their social-emotional well-being as well as their academic performance, creating a more supportive and inclusive atmosphere.

Supporting a culture that actively values and seeks out feedback means we must welcome and encourage questions from our students. Wait time after a question is asked, whether initiated by the teacher or a student, is important. Students need time to think and share their thoughts. Turn and Talk and Think-Ink-Pair-Share are two protocols that encourage more participation and active involvement in class discussions to help students track and continue to revise their thinking. The latter is especially effective for fostering question makers because it ensures that everyone is accountable for getting their thoughts down so they can share with a partner or small group. Writing down their thinking in a reflection journal allows students to easily update their thoughts based on discussion with others time. Developing a spirit of inquiry and a sense of wonder is important for students, as these traits translate into the cultivation of lifelong learners, whether from books, travel, or connection with others. Today, more than ever, we need to produce global citizens who are adaptable and open to sharing their thoughts with others, who learn through practiced reflection how to be constructively critical and analytical, and who strive to let go of biases and narrow worldviews.

Assessment and Reflection

Collecting data on student understanding is a form of gathering feedback from students on what they have learned and what they still need to understand. Such feedback can guide you to focus on what to teach next and how to teach it. The best teachers take time to continuously assess students throughout their lessons. Formative assessment is supported by decades of research and thousands of studies that demonstrate its value not just for powerful student performance outcomes but also for accelerating student growth (Black & Wiliam, 2010; Hattie, 2009; Popham, 2018).

Assessing as you go requires minute-by-minute reflection. It requires that teachers continually ask themselves three questions:

- *What do my students know?*
- *What do my students need?*
- *How do I teach it?*

These three questions are essential to making decisions about whether students are ready to progress to the next stages or steps or if they first need to revisit learning and clear up misconceptions. Researchers refer to formative assessment as feedback because it provides information about students' status to help teachers decide what to pursue next. The three questions are so important that Pérsida asks her teacher education candidates to chant them in sequence repeatedly to reinforce how necessary they are to achieving student success.

The 3-2-1 Strategy

The 3-2-1 Strategy is a useful and versatile technique for formative assessment that can apply to any content area. The beauty of the strategy is its flexible nature and ability to engage K–12 students with text actively and meaningfully. The framework is simple: students respond to prompts that ask for three responses to one prompt, two to the next, and finally, one response.

Teachers can tailor the prompts to suit the content or skills being taught. In social studies, for example, the teacher might ask students to summarize three big ideas gleaned from the text, share two insights about what aspects of their reading were most interesting to them, and pose one question about the text. During writing time, students might list three things they tried today, two questions they are still wondering about, and one thing they will try in the next writing session. They could also record the title and author of a book in their reader's notebook and write about three things they discovered while reading the book, two interesting or surprising things, and one question they have for the author or another reader. In science, students might write about three things they observed, two questions they have, and one hypothesis or conclusion they made. Another way to use 3-2-1 is to compare responses written after the first lesson in a unit of study with responses during the last part of the unit to help students evaluate how their understanding of a concept developed over time. Some general frameworks for the 3-2-1 Strategy appear in Figure 5.3.

Figure 5.3
Sample Approaches Using the 3-2-1 Strategy

3	things you discovered
2	interesting sentences from your writing or a peer's writing
1	question you might have
3	keywords
2	new writing topics, formats, or strategies
1	idea to think about and possibly develop
3	differences between ___________ and ___________
2	effects of ___________ on ___________
1	insight about yourself as a learner
3	things you learned
2	things that confirmed what you already knew
1	strategy you will try when you revise
3	things that went well during workshop time
2	choices you made today that helped you move forward as a writer
1	problem that you solved or that remains unsolved

The 3-2-1 Strategy gives students a voice in class routines and provides immediate feedback that they can use to make adjustments as they progress with the lesson. Sharing what they know and don't know helps the teacher provide more support by differentiating instruction or reteaching. Using this framework as an exit slip for final reflections is a way to bring closure to any learning experience, regardless of age level or content area, and allows you to look for patterns and trends related to students' understanding of the content and skills learned.

The Important Thing Protocol

For another method of scaffolding student reflection that was especially pertinent to younger elementary students, Lynne developed a protocol called The Important Thing (see Appendix S). She drew inspiration from *The Important Book,* a picture book by Margaret Wise Brown, to devise a framework that prompts students to write about their learning. The scaffold, which is simple enough for everyone to use and appropriate in any content area, asks students to identify what in their learning was most important, interesting, and surprising to them and share their thinking with their teacher and their classmates. After reading the book aloud in class, Lynne modeled using the scaffold to reflect on lessons and units of study. With older students, she extended the protocol by asking them to expand on each big idea, with descriptions, examples, explanations, or even a quote.

The Daily Dozen Protocol

Jen's 7th grade science class was always a beehive of activity. Students watched video clips related to their lessons, wrote in their science journals, conducted experiments, and often rotated through various workstations to observe and take notes. Students were always in perpetual motion; after all, 43-minute periods were never enough time.

The introduction of so many Tier 3 vocabulary words created an obstacle for some students. They needed to be able to readily explain their observations and the phenomena they were studying using appropriate vocabulary. Often, the last few minutes of class time were devoted to reminders about assignments and upcoming quizzes and tests. Jen and Lynne discussed the class's need for closure to help students reflect on the day's lesson and solidify their learning. Together, they generated a list of prompts for students to capture their experiences in a quick three- to five-minute activity (see Appendix T). The written reflection not only made students' thinking more permanent but also meant they could review their thoughts at the beginning of the next class for greater continuity in their learning.

A Teacher's Take

There are countless other ways to gain snapshots of students' learning status. Here, Beverly DeRise, a teacher at The Janus School, shares a simple adjustment she's made related to homework.

Turning Barriers into Bridges

Fourth grade teacher Greg Moll asked us a question that might resonate with you: "How do I find the time to fit reflection in, and what do I need to do?" Greg had tried some reflection protocols to see how they would work with his math students. He explained:

> I was really surprised when I read the responses students gave to the Neuro-Reflection Protocol, and I could see thinking from them I hadn't seen before. Struggling students knew exactly where their thinking got tangled, and they wrote about how they handled or didn't handle it. I was amazed. But I just don't know how to allot reflection the time it needs. And that was only one protocol. It's just overwhelming.

Greg's concern is valid and shared by many. It takes *time* to read, understand, and incorporate new strategies and approaches, such as reflection, into our teaching. Making changes can feel overwhelming and downright painful. But what if we shifted our thinking and found a way to start prioritizing reflection? Here's a simple, three-part plan:

1. Make one change.
2. Get rid of the "tomato suckers."
3. Reflect, reframe, and restore.

Make One Change

This is our first piece of advice. Think about one thing you've read that resonates with you and begin there. Maybe you want to try a specific protocol after you complete your next unit, or perhaps you want to incorporate reflection journaling into your class's routine. Those are both good and worthy places to begin. Remember: Rome wasn't built in a day, every masterpiece was once a work in progress, and everything comes in its own time. Catherine often refers to these familiar sayings to remind herself and her students that success may not be immediate, but if we put effort into taking small, deliberate steps, we *will* accomplish what we set out to do. What one change will you make? Write it down. Tell a coworker about it. Write in your reflection journal about it. Find your way past a single barrier to build a bridge to connect your current practice with new possibilities.

Get Rid of the Tomato Suckers

This is our advice for finding time to incorporate reflection into your day. Catherine's husband, Steve, learned a bit of wisdom years ago from Ruth, a spunky 80-plus-year-old friend who, like him, enjoyed planting heirloom tomatoes. When she visited during the summer, she and Steve would stand around the tomatoes for long periods of time, inspecting the plants and talking about the soil and the weather. She shared what she had learned as a farm girl from Lancaster County. Steve, too, had grown up on a farm, but Ruth shared something about tomatoes that no one had before: "Steve, it's like this. The roots are fibrous and shallow, so that's why the plant needs support as it grows. The main stem here, kinda like Route 30, is the main highway for nutrients and hydration to get to the leaves and branches. You gotta take off those tomato suckers, though. Let me show you what I mean."

Ruth pointed to one of the small shoots growing between the leaf and the main stem. "Now, these are the suckers. They're like little armpits of the plant. Keep 'em, and the plant will get bushy and make lots of small fruit. I don't recommend that. Remove those suckers, and your tomato plant will be nice and tame, and it'll give less fruit, but those tomatoes for your BLTs will be larger."

This story is an agricultural parable. If teaching is a tomato plant, and all the expectations and demands are the branches, only *you* can evaluate which ones are the tomato suckers—the time suckers in your day that need to be pruned. They may have some benefit, but in the whole scheme of things, they may be taking up valuable time that could go toward reflection.

Try this exercise: First, list everything your class does in a day or a week. Then, read over the list. Which tasks must stay? Which are the nonnegotiables? The list will no doubt be long, but chances are you'll find some things that *seem* important and *may* produce fruit, but you don't *need* to do them.

Those are the tomato suckers. If you prune them away, you may come to realize that they weren't that important after all. Replace those tasks with reflection opportunities for your students. Instead of a big, bushy tomato plant that produces lots of little fruit, your refocused energy will get you and the students bigger and better results.

In Chapter 6, we'll talk more about reflecting on barriers to teaching effectiveness and then reframing and restoring them to what you want them to be.

Final Thoughts on Intentional Design for Reflection

Building reflection into your classroom and your teaching isn't easy. It takes a lot of practice. Developing students who are skilled in the art of reflection never happens all at once; it happens over time. But it isn't accidental; it takes persistence and a boatload of patience. If your students' initial attempts at reflection fall short of the mark, don't give up. With repeated opportunities to share their reflections, they will improve over time. Daily reflection will help them imagine possibilities for their learning and make choices for independent writing, reading, and research that are sensible and meaningful. Helping students develop a growth mindset, with which they both welcome challenges and expect struggle, will lead them to become thinkers who make sage decisions. Opportunities to make choices and engage in self-reflection are essential for students to grow their critical-thinking skills and tackle the daily challenges presented over the course of both the academic day and real life.

Questions for Individual Reflection

1. How can you prioritize your students' needs, goals, and challenges?
2. How can you encourage your students to become question makers, take responsible risks, and be more comfortable with reflection?
3. What questions are still lingering?
4. How can you collaborate with other educators to find multiple pathways to reflective practice for your students?
5. What opportunities do you have to model reflective practice for your students?
6. How does reflective practice embrace the opportunity to try and fail without repercussion? How can you teach students that failures lead to success over time?

Questions to Discuss with Colleagues

1. How can you make your classroom a safer and more welcoming space for students?
2. How do you foster a sense of belonging?
3. What are some steps you could take to promote a growth mindset for you and your students?
4. When can you build in time for student reflection?
6. How can you create a culture of support and joy while fostering high expectations for your students? How often do you model or demonstrate a growth mindset for your students?

6

Making Time for Teacher Reflection

Using self-reflection to improve your teaching relies on a growth mindset and a commitment to lifelong learning: these are both values that, when passed on to students, empower them to set their own goals and take ownership of their learning process.

—*Carol S. Dweck*

It's a widely shared truth that the most valuable resource a high-quality school has is its staff. Although the primary focus of this book is the importance of giving students the time and tools to reflect on their learning, it is also essential for teachers to reflect on their own practices and model reflection for their students. No matter what type of educator you are, reflection provides an opportunity to review the outcome of a lesson or a meeting, determine next steps for instruction or implementation, and record your thoughts about how to adjust or deepen understanding based on the formative and summative data you collected. Research highlights that teacher reflection is closely linked to improved instructional practices and student outcomes (Larrivee, 2000; Schön, 1983). Teacher reflection also plays a crucial role in professional development. Engaging in reflective practices allows educators to assess and refine their teaching methods, leading to better student outcomes. For instance, microteaching—in which teachers record and then review their lessons—has an effect size of 0.88, highlighting its effectiveness in enhancing teaching practices (Hattie, 2009). Likewise, according to Dewey (1933), reflective thinking enables teachers to transform routine action into intelligent action as they question and evaluate their own decisions. Thus, reflection is a critical component of professional growth and student-centered teaching.

Teachers record their reflections in various ways, but it's wise to commit to a simple and direct method for preserving your thoughts so you can use them to inform future lessons. Teachers can take notes on their lesson plans or file lesson materials with date-stamped sticky notes bearing thoughts about how the lesson went. It's important to capture the reflections in the moment or soon after to keep them from getting lost. Zeichner and Liston (1996) emphasize that maintaining written reflective records, whether in journals or annotated lesson plans, supports the development of a reflective habit and contributes to a deeper awareness of one's pedagogical choices. Boud and colleagues (1985) suggest that the act of written reflection not only aids memory but also enhances metacognitive processes, allowing teachers to revisit and refine their instructional strategies over time.

When Aileen taught high school English, she sometimes taught the same text year after year (e.g., Langston Hughes's poetry in English 10). She realizes now she could have saved time and increased her instructional effectiveness by recording students' responses to certain aspects of the unit in the moment instead of making the same "instructional choices" (read: errors) for multiple years because she didn't remember the previous year's insights. When Aileen returned to lesson plans or texts that *did* contain contemporary reflections, it was almost as if she had found a coach to support her teaching. The written reflections helped her adjust her lesson to incorporate what she had learned the previous year. When you take time to preserve your thinking, not only do you preserve details that can serve to strengthen future lessons, but you also allow yourself the opportunity to return to those notes with a more experienced and informed lens.

Of course, teacher reflection enhances instruction in all content areas. How students respond to a science lab, an explanation of how to solve a math equation, or a list of the questions that students asked in a social studies lesson is extremely important feedback for guiding subsequent teaching or curricular choices. Teaching is not just about covering the scope and sequence; it's also about addressing students' curiosities and misunderstandings. This is the heart of teaching—and reflection is a core component of effective teaching practices.

Just as we model reading and writing for our students, we need to model reflection behaviors to encourage them to incorporate reflection into their own lives. Thinking about our own thinking and our teaching practices helps us to grow as educators by reflecting on the choices we've made regarding lesson design, lesson improvement, and opportunities for student engagement.

Students admire teachers who "walk the walk," making it evident that they, too, are involved in the process of deep reflection. For example, a teacher might think aloud during a lesson to share their process, saying, *Wow, these are great questions you're asking. I'm going to write them down to use next year when I teach this lesson* or *The rotations we used for this lab didn't work out the way I had hoped. I really appreciate your flexibility today. I'm going to make a note on my lesson plan to remind myself of what happened. What ideas do you have that would have helped the lab run more effectively?* This kind of modeling helps students see reflection as a real, worthwhile activity, not just something assigned to them. They also learn that opportunities to make choices and engage in self-reflection are essential for both teachers and students.

Reflection in Your Professional Life

As teachers, our professional lives grow and change for the better when we learn to make reflection an everyday habit. Reflection can take place after a lesson, during your planning period, or at the end of the day. It can also be effective to reflect before you start teaching. The most important thing is to build in a time for reflection that works best for you. You might want to set an alarm to remind yourself to take a few minutes; it doesn't have to take a lot of time. We don't recommend creating a document that will be too cumbersome to read the following year. That type of complexity sets up an unnecessary obstacle to overcome.

Reflection can also be used to process ideas that do not need to be revisited. Once you decide the best strategy, format, and timing for you to engage in reflection, commit to practicing until it becomes a part of your routine. In *Atomic Habits* (2018), James Clear states, "On average, it takes more than two months before a new behavior becomes automatic—66 days to be exact. And how long it takes a new habit to form can vary widely depending on the behavior, the person, and the circumstances" (p. 66). Just as we tell our students that practice helps us become better and more acclimated to a behavior, we need to tell ourselves. Allow your students to help you meet your goal by sharing how hard you are working on building the habit of reflection. A student-led cheering squad may hasten your success.

The RESET Reflection Wall Protocol

An old proverb says, "If you want to go fast, go alone. If you want to go far, go together." This adage applies to the power of a group reflecting together. The

RESET Reflection Wall Protocol (see Appendix U) uses chart paper, sticky notes, and the RESET acronym—Revisit the bright spots; Evaluate the challenges, problems, and solutions; Shifts in perspective; Effort that mattered; and Tomorrow's intentions—to guide a team of teachers through reflecting on any aspect of instruction, using the visual representation in front of them as an anchor for rich discussion. Some of the reflection questions in the protocol relate to an end-of-year review, but it can be used at any time.

Classroom Snapshot: A Team's RESET Reflection

When a team has worked alongside one another for years, its members sometimes assume they know what everyone thinks about everything. But a year-end reflection using the RESET Reflection Wall Protocol can be revelatory. What Catherine and her grade-level team had intended to be a quick 15-minute share time turned into more.

"It was a special time," said a colleague. "It felt like we built more trust for one another." Everyone was being honest and vulnerable, encouraging one another, sharing new ideas, and collecting inspiration for improving aspects of their teaching. Yes, it was the end of the school year, and they were all tired and eager to finish cleaning their classrooms and officially begin summer break, but the authentic, valuable, and meaningful space they created for reflection that day kept everyone enthralled.

They started out with chart paper and sticky notes, and the wall quickly filled up with observations and successes (see Figure 6.1).

Revisiting the bright spots of the year brought out joy. Catherine's grade-level partner, Ursula Gamler, reflected on the nonfiction reading and writing unit she had co-designed with Catherine: "Hard-to-reach students were excited and engaged!" Catherine agreed, saying, "When student research reports, posters, and poetry to go along with it were displayed in the hallway, the kids felt so proud, and I did, too." Greg Moll reflected on his science unit: "The chain reaction project was a huge success." The team acknowledged that these lessons had pulled in even the most reluctant students. It was reason to celebrate the progress students had made and connections that had formed between teachers and students.

The tone of the conversation turned more serious as the team moved on to evaluating challenges. "Dealing with student behavior was overwhelming this year," Ursula volunteered. The group grew quiet. Everyone felt the weight of those words. Greg shared that he had struggled with student engagement during social studies and wanted to rethink his approach to the subject. Catherine noted that she often jumped into learning too quickly in the morning. "Next year," she said, "I want to spend more time doing what I hear Ursula and Greg do with their classes—share a joke of the day, an inspiring story, a video. I know these are community-building times that give students a chance to ease into their day. It's also a time for them to get to know me better."

Figure 6.1

Example: Year-End RESET Reflection Wall

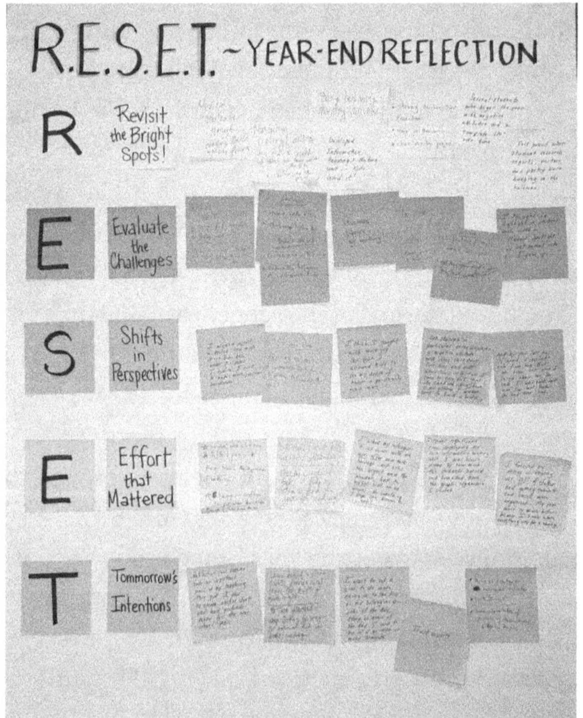

The shifts in perspective discussion generated valuable insight. Greg altered his valuation of anchor charts: "My thinking has shifted about anchor charts. I decided to keep a running chart throughout the unit that contains content, vocabulary, and mystery ideas. It worked." Ursula shared that she'd let go of something that wasn't working: "Instead of obsessing over what I was 'supposed to do' during intervention time, I created meaningful activities that worked."

This discussion about shifts in thinking provided the team with a natural segue into considering the facets of their teaching they had invested in and the dividends it had earned them. Greg had been intentional about guiding his students to reflect more in math. Ursula was pleased that she had put time and effort into matching kids with the right books, knowing it contributes to a love of reading: "It isn't easy, and it takes time," she said. "But it's worth it."

Team members next talked about their intentions for the year ahead. Ursula saw the need to restructure how she disseminates important information to parents. Greg wanted to deepen reflection in his classroom by using daily math journals. Catherine also spoke about reflection and the meaning it had taken on in her classroom: "Reflection has become such an important part of my teaching. I want it to be a habit for me and for my students. My goal is to post anchor charts with reflection questions throughout the room."

Although the meeting lasted longer than the intended 15-minute check-in, everyone agreed it was time well spent. They wrapped up the conversation and the school year having experienced the power of shared reflection, the kind that reminded them they were in this together, the kind that helped them reset for the year ahead.

The Reflect, Reframe, Restore Protocol

Taking inventory of practices that are keeping them from being highly effective enables teachers to get out of ruts that are preventing them from moving forward toward success. The Reflect, Reframe, Restore Protocol (see Appendix V) is an effective tool for teachers to use when they are trying to move past any kind of barrier in their teaching practice. Figure 6.2 shows the responses of Emily, an elementary classroom teacher who was frustrated by her students' struggles to follow directions and transition during the day. Her willingness to pause and be honest with herself led to a monumental shift in her thinking.

Emily shared with us that she followed through on talking with the teacher she mentioned in her reflection. When they sat down together, Emily was surprised to find that the veteran teacher was open about the fact that she, too, had struggled with classroom management early in her career. She affirmed Emily's plan to take one small step of focusing on an area of concern, such as making the transition from one activity to another, and guide her students to mastery of that chosen transition. She invited Emily to meet with her regularly to process ideas together. In this case, Emily's courage to be honest with herself about a professional struggle not only led to her finding new tools and strategies to move her students away from unwanted behaviors but also opened the door to a new professional relationship that would provide a safe place to process her thinking. It was a professional community that formed naturally—a relationship teachers truly need and desire.

Reflection in Your Personal Life

Reflection will become more of a habit in professional life if it becomes a strong habit in personal life. Of course, time is a factor here. But educators shouldn't think about reflection as a chore, like the two- to three-page "Reflection" section at the end of a graduate school paper. Reflection can happen as you are getting ready for work, during your commute, and even during recess or bus duty. It can be informal or more intentional, such as a written journal or meeting with a mentor or colleague to talk through some thoughts. Reflection enables educators to slow down just enough to remember what we want to remember—minimizing those "forgetful moments" that sometimes plague us—and to recollect what's important to us and required of us. More to the point, reflection helps the important things stay memorable so that we can cherish them more readily.

Tools to Capture the Data: Student and Colleague Feedback

There are as many ways to reflect as there are ways to take one's coffee. And, just like a coffee order, there's no way that is best for everyone—it's just what's best for the person ordering the coffee or doing the reflecting.

It's important to consider how much time you have to engage in consistent reflection, your purpose for reflection (there can be more than one), and what format feels most natural to you. Some teachers might start a reflection journal—or two, if they want to keep both a professional and a personal journal. Many designate space for recording their reflections in their planners, adding a function to a tool already in use. Others might record their reflections as voice memos and save them on their electronic device. If you do this, make sure to title and date the voice memo clearly so that you can find what you are looking for if you need to revisit your thoughts.

Gathering feedback from students or colleagues about our teaching is another tool to foster reflection. Having students complete a quick survey or asking a peer or trusted instructional coach to provide feedback after an

Figure 6.2

Example: Emily's Response to the Reflect, Reframe, Restore Protocol

Reflect

Describe in detail an area of your teaching that is especially difficult, challenging, or frustrating.

- Name the difficulty, challenge, or problem. *I've been feeling overwhelmed by my lack of classroom control for some time. I'm to the point where I start to feel anxious when I arrive at school because I know it's going to be tough, no matter what.*
- What is the narrative you have been telling yourself? Is it accurate? *Students don't respect me, and honestly, it feels accurate.*
- What is in your realm of power or control? What is not? *I can control the strategies I try and my reactions to students' behaviors. I can't actually control their behavior!*
- How or where do you feel stuck? *I want a calm, respectful classroom, but I can't seem to figure it out. I've tried different ideas I've seen on social media, but they may work for a short time, and then I'm back to where I started.*
- What emotions are involved? *Fear, dread, anxiety, defeat*

Reframe

As you think about the difficulty, challenge, or problem, begin to imagine it through a different, more constructive lens.

- I wonder if the problem is really about... *students not understanding my expectations.*
- If I were to stand in someone else's shoes, I would... *see that I don't always follow through.*
- What would happen if I modified... *my attitude toward my struggles and asking for help.*
- A pattern that has emerged is... *I need help but I'm too embarrassed to ask for it.*
- One thing I'm doing well, despite the challenge, is... *There are many things I do well!*
- A resource or trusted colleague who could help me with this is... *Candace down the hall. She seems to have it together when it comes to classroom management.*
- I realize now that... *I need to reframe my struggle or I'll stay stuck in it!*

Restore

When teaching gets hard, it's easy to feel stuck in what feels broken, lost, or unclear. Describe how you can rebuild what is broken, re-establish what is lost, and redefine what is unclear. Ground yourself in a new possibility.

- A boundary to establish is... *We run the entire classroom in an orderly way.*
- I know now that... *it's wise to take one small step at time. I'll start by focusing on how students enter the room.*
- Hopes and dreams I have for this are... *I'm going to have a class meeting tomorrow to discuss what entering the room will look like, sound like, and feel like when they arrive the following day. By the end of the month, we'll start class on time, with everyone in their seat.*
- I believe the solution lies in... *getting students' buy-in and taking time to practice the behavior so that expectations are clear.*
- It's possible that... *with support and calm, deliberate effort, we'll establish some new norms for conduct. Even as I write this, I feel a small sense of relief knowing I am taking steps toward a better classroom experience for my students and myself.*

observation helps build a habit of inquiry and reflection. When we realize that this type of feedback promotes reflection and learning, it feels less like criticism. It's more a way to move past feeling stuck or an opportunity to breathe life into a lesson or activity we have been teaching for a long time. Don't assume that reflection is always generated internally; external insights and inspiration can bring about the best type of reflection!

In Lynne's work as a writing coach, she often used a combination observation form and rubric (see Figure 6.3) to help her determine which components of a writing workshop were present on a regular basis and which components were rarely observed or seemed to be absent. Over the course of two to three weeks, this chart helped Lynne reflect on what she needed to model or team-teach with the teacher and what questions she could ask the teacher as they conferred and reflected on their practices as writing teachers. Her conferences with student writers also helped her ensure the components included in Figure 6.3 were used in each writing workshop.

Renewal: Each Year Is a Different One

When Lynne returned to her classroom after attending the West Chester Writing Project invitational summer institute on the teaching of writing, she remembered the words of her facilitators. Bob and Lois had advised them to "think big, but start small," echoing the sentiments of the guru of change theory, Michael Fullan. Lynne wanted to try so much, but she knew she needed to be patient and think about one or two goals that would focus her efforts when she returned to her 4th graders.

Lynne decided that keeping her own writer's notebook and asking her students to do the same were worthy goals and closely related. She could model with her own notebook and show her students how her notebook was a place to gather writing topics and to practice author's craft. The following year, she tackled writing workshops and writing minilessons that followed the gradual release model but were tied to a mentor text. The next year was devoted to portfolio assessment, and then, to other formative assessment measures. Lynne's experience with the five-week summer writing institute at West Chester University, followed by a second institute experience at the University of Pennsylvania, provided long-term goals for the next five years.

In the decades that followed, Lynne tackled questions that would help her continue to set goals and imagine the possibilities for each new school year. Here are some reflection questions she often returns to, year after year:

- *What are the underlying structures that support my teaching?*
- *Am I using them effectively?*
- *What are the organizational structures and routines that help students smoothly transition from one subject or activity to the next? Any additions? Tweaks? What worked? What didn't work? Why?*
- *What are the mechanisms and procedures used to communicate with my grade-level colleagues, reading specialists, ML teachers, coaches, and parents? Are there areas for improvement?*
- *How can I capitalize on opportunities for my students to connect with me and with one another?*
- *How can I build in time for daily reflection?*
- *What classroom routines support partnership and collaboration?*
- *How do I promote and encourage collaboration?*
- *How can I help my students develop the art of reflection?*
- *Am I modeling reflective practices across the content areas?*
- *How do I monitor and document my students' growth and interactions with the new programs I am required to implement? What are my thoughts and feelings about these new programs?*
- *Is my record-keeping system (daily formative assessment) working for me? Does it need to be streamlined to make it more user-friendly?*
- *What part do I play as a teacher leader in my school and school district?*
- *How can I help new teachers with school initiatives? How can I help them feel comfortable and part of the school culture?*
- *What about my classroom library? Do I need to do some weeding? How can I involve my students in the selection of books that will add to and energize my current collection?*
- *What am I doing to promote self-care? How will I schedule in time for me to exercise, write professionally, read for pleasure, experiment with watercolor, take some art classes, and so on?*
- *How am I connecting with my colleagues (remembering to smile as they pass me in the hallway, trying to eat lunch two or three times a week with grade-level partners and other members of my school community)?*
- *How diverse, equitable, and inclusive is my classroom? My school?*
- *How can I support the shared decision-making process in my building?*
- *How can I encourage my colleagues to make their voices heard?*

Figure 6.3
Template: Observation Sheet and Rubric for Writing Workshops

Component	Teacher A	Teacher B	Teacher C	Teacher D	Teacher E
Use of stages: prewriting, drafting, revising, editing, publishing, sharing					
Modeling by teacher, samples from literature, and/or student samples					
Use of a writer's notebook to write observations, make lists, find topics, study craft					
Conferences (teacher-student as formal or informal such as roving conference)					
Partners or peer response groups are used for conferring					
Long, daily chunks of time for writing, individually or collaboratively					
Students are asked to engage in reflection (built-in time at end of workshop daily)					
Choice of topic and freedom to abandon to start anew					
Use of well-timed, compact focus lessons following GRRM					
Formative assessment measures and self-evaluation practices observed					

Rubric

Components	Ideal	Acceptable	Unacceptable
Use of stages: prewriting, drafting, revising, editing, publishing, sharing	All parts of process observable in workshop—through teacher instruction or student actions	Most parts of the process observable in some form	Students and teacher do not refer to writing process in any noticeable way
Modeling by teacher, samples from literature, and/or student samples	Teacher uses her own writing to model as well as student models or models from real literature	Teacher uses student models from the present class or others or uses models from literature	No modeling is used during writing workshop
Conferences (teacher-student as formal or informal)	Roving conference or formal writing conference based on teacher observations, student requests, and status of the class	Whole-group conferences to assist some students with an aspect of their writing process	No conferences are used during writing workshop
Peer response groups	Students belong to a trusted response group and share their writing to receive praise and polish	Students share their writing with a partner; students offer help with spelling or other editing matters	No peer response groups are used during writing workshop
Long, daily chunks of time for sustained writing, individually or collaboratively	Writing every day during workshop time for 15–40 minutes, depending on age of students	Long chunks of writing time are offered two or three times a week	Little or no writing time is evidenced
Choice of writing topic and freedom to abandon and start anew	Writing workshop offers students a choice in topics and the freedom to abandon a piece and start anew	A balance of teacher-chosen topics and student-chosen topics, and some choice within teacher-assigned topics	Teacher choice of topic; assigned pieces must be completed
Use of well-timed, compact minilessons	Strategy-based minilessons are 5–10 minutes, unless presented in an interactive format with student participation	Strategy-based mini-lessons are presented	There is no observable evidence of direct instruction during writing workshop
Assessment and self-evaluation	Student work is assessed through process and product; students reflect on process and product	Work is often assessed through process and product; students know how to reflect but don't engage in reflection	Product only is assessed; students do not engage in reflective practice

Final Thoughts on Reflective Practices for Teachers

Reflective practice supports the work we already do with our students in our classrooms. Tovani (2011) shares her thinking with us in her book on assessment: "If we expand our definition and consider how we use it [assessment] to our advantage, we don't have to breathlessly await state test results in hopes that our students showed growth. We can take matters into our own hands if we are willing to include and use what we see and hear in our classrooms every day as data" (p. 151). Reflection is the tool that allows us to take matters into our own hands.

In an article titled "Why Teachers Must Become Change Agents," Fullan (1993b) states that every person in a learning organization is a change agent and thus is charged with responsibility for making continual improvements and helping to foster individual and collective inquiry and a process of continuous renewal. Without individual action and reaction to alter learning environments rather than maintaining the status quo, there is no chance for profound change. According to Fullan again, in *Change Forces* (1993a), "Moral purpose needs an engine, and that engine is individual, skilled change agents pushing for changes around them" (p. 40). There is nothing more powerful than reflection to plant the seeds of change.

Teacher reflection is often closely linked with goals and learning targets. Setting and monitoring our progress toward achieving our professional goals will ensure our effectiveness and help us reach our full potential. Reflection should be motivating and engaging; the form of reflection we create for ourselves should be specific, concise, and instructive. It should empower us to take responsible risks, to grow and change as educators. Taking time to reflect on how a lesson went, specifically how students responded in ways that surprised and excited us, can help us make decisions about how we structure our classroom environment, our instruction, and our assessments. Reflecting on practice also helps us develop stronger relationships with our colleagues and students as we make choices that will transform lives and, eventually, our world for the better. Sharing our reflections with colleagues is a way to celebrate our diverse talents, abilities, and cultures.

A Teacher's Take

Fourth grade teacher Ursula Gamler has come to see reflection as not just useful but necessary: "If we don't reflect, we don't become as good as we can be . . . our kids don't become as good as they can be."

If we are to focus on developing growth mindsets in our students, we must take the lead ourselves, as lifelong learners. Embracing a reflective practice promotes a culture of inquiry and boosts teacher morale and motivation when we begin to see the positive impact of our efforts. Purposeful reflection takes time, practice, and commitment. It is a valuable way to focus on our own improvement and keep alive our sense of curiosity and wonder. Teaching is a difficult profession, yet perhaps one of the most rewarding. Classroom teachers need to spend time reflecting on what they value as members of the teaching profession and for the students in their classrooms. We also must understand that we need to value reflection as a process and a journey as much as we value the destination.

Questions for Individual Reflection

1. How do you learn? (reflection as a magnifying lens, or meaning making)
2. How has your thinking changed? (reflection as a mirror, or metacognition)
3. How are you growing as a learner? What are your next steps? (reflection as a map, or metastrategic thinking)
4. How can collaboration with grade-level peers, content-area colleagues, coaches, and administrators further support or enhance the work you do?
5. What barriers need to be removed so that you can make reflection an everyday habit as a professional educator?

Questions to Discuss with Colleagues

1. Reflect on why you became a teacher. What are some changes you would like to make to your daily routines, teaching methods, or school culture? How can you act as a catalyst for these changes?
2. What prevents educators from finding the time to reflect? What is some practical advice to help overcome each obstacle?

3. Why is it important for educators to reflect on their own practice?
4. How does reflection propel us toward learning?
5. How can your ability to reflect in both your personal and professional lives benefit your students? How can you weave the work of reflection into your daily or weekly routine?
6. What steps can you take to create a learning environment that fosters reflection as a habit?
7. Take some time to reflect on what you value and believe about how reflections on assessments can be used to help students be more successful. Make a list and discuss with grade-level colleagues.

Afterword

Now that you've reached the end of our book, we hope you can imagine the possibilities of effectively and authentically incorporating reflection into your current teaching practice. Over time, the scaffolds and protocols here will become as automatic to you as "turn and talk," and you'll see how reflection positively affects your students' attitude toward learning and makes their thinking more sophisticated. A routine of reflective practice allows your students to take ownership of their learning and gives you feedback you can use to monitor and adjust your teaching. In the end, reflective practice creates self-aware and responsible students who are knowledgeable about how they learn and are equipped with key skills and strategies to become lifelong learners.

As you begin to think about a classroom where reflection is an integral part of every day, you might wonder what your first steps should be. Teachers who embrace reflective practice embark on a journey that asks them to tailor learning experiences to fit students' needs, self-question, discuss learning experiences and challenges with colleagues, and set goals and self-assess. As you draw on your own strengths, always remember to observe the best practices of your colleagues and mentors and apply them to your own teaching. It's a good idea to confide in a trusted colleague or group of educators who can cheer you on, offering encouragement and support. Finding colleagues to collaborate, share your thinking aloud, and design and try out protocols with is essential—and you'll also help one another develop and maintain a positive mindset. Your cheering squad need not consist only of members of your grade-level team or even those in your building or district. Think bigger—perhaps you could share with a colleague in a local chapter of your state literacy organization, a participant in your National Writing Project summer institute, or a classmate in your graduate classes. Collaboration will deepen your understanding and provide food for thought.

Establishing opportunities for students to reflect also helps us better understand how they think and see themselves as learners. The most effective reflections are multidimensional, involving thought with breadth and depth that is more than superficial. Often students have revised their thoughts in response to their thinking being challenged or supported.

In our collective experience as educators, we have worked with all types of learners—from primary to collegiate, from native English speakers to multilanguage learners, and in socioeconomically disadvantaged neighborhoods as well as communities of affluence. We know one thing is true for all of them: they almost never take time for reflection unless prompted. And without reflection, valuable knowledge slips away into the abyss.

As educators in K–12 classrooms, we can take responsibility for carving out time to think about our thinking, our decisions and plans for improvement, our long- and short-term goals, and the pathways we choose to reach our destinations. We help our students by giving them sentence starters and prompts to ignite their thinking, asking them to record their big ideas in a journal, and providing myriad protocols and scaffolds to stimulate their thoughts and revision efforts. We use anchor charts to make the thinking of the learning community visible, permanent, and yet ongoing. Teachers use anchor charts to model how to set important, achievable goals. In other words, we help students engage in higher-order thinking and prepare them to evaluate their own thought processes.

The three metaphors we have shared in our book help develop reflective practitioners in our classrooms, beginning as early as kindergarten and continuing long after they leave our classrooms as parents, spouses, and global citizens in our workforce. This multifaceted approach to effective reflection is a practical framework at any level:

- **Meaning making (reflection as a magnifying glass)**—Learners process new information, analyze it, summarize it, and repackage it to construct understanding (Kramer Ertel, 2021). Unprocessed information is quickly forgotten.
- **Metacognition (reflection as a mirror)**—Learners think about their own thinking, evaluate learning strategies, and adjust approaches to improve (Hallstead & Nash, 2020). Metacognitive strategies have a significant impact on learning outcomes (Hattie, 2009).
- **Metastrategic thinking (reflection as a map)**—Learners engage in big-picture planning, problem solving, and decision making to guide future actions. This type of thinking is essential for innovation and problem solving in real-world contexts (Iordanou, 2022).

Making big changes in the quality of student reflection and the ease with which students navigate the scaffolds and protocols we recommend in our book does not happen overnight. It's essential to provide daily time for reflection and model, model, model! Celebrate the smallest steps your students take to use reflection to make meaning out of new information, think about their own thinking, and set goals to improve and grow.

Reflection offers exciting pathways for engaging students in learning throughout the academic day and promises the chance for each of them to be part of their own educational journey—to take ownership of the process and actively participate in charting their course. As educators, our goal is to teach students how to learn and how to evaluate their learning, not just what to learn. Reflective practices play a big part in this endeavor. Cultivating a reflective community is possible only if we provide opportunities for reflection, prioritize opportunities to share thinking with others, and consider changing or adding to our thinking in some small way as a result.

Reflection and Multilingual Learners: Major Takeaways

Learning new content and articulating understandings in a non-primary language is obviously more challenging than in your stronger language. This means that teachers need to deliberately frame opportunities for MLs to reflect on their learning. Helping MLs closely reflect on a lesson (reflection as a magnifying glass), understand how they can best tackle their learning (reflection as a mirror), and plan for success (reflection as a map) can make the difference in achieving success.

The reflection protocols included in this book serve as both a scaffold for students and a window for teachers. They get MLs revisiting content, focusing on what is most important, and demonstrating understanding by distilling their learning into quick summaries and deeper analyses. Protocols provide MLs a second structured opportunity to pick up what they might have missed due to the language of delivery. For teachers, reflection protocols provide visual evidence of learning—additional formative data they can use to address misunderstandings.

Additionally, many of this book's reflection protocols are designed to be empowering—to help students take more ownership of their learning. The benefits of empowerment to our MLs cannot be minimized, given the linguistic challenges they face on a minute by minute basis.

We know that adding reflection to learning will not fix all the problems that exist in our current educational climate, but we believe it can help immensely. We cannot afford to keep reflection on the back burner, as it has been for decades, with just a few educators knowing about and experiencing the benefits of reflective practice for their students. It's time to give it the attention it deserves and make it a key part of learning. When we do, we know that it will "spill over" into other areas of students' lives, empowering them to think deeply, act with intention, and take ownership of their learning.

When we share our reflections about teaching practices and student growth, relationships become positive and demonstrate mutual respect. Students feel they are an integral part of the learning cycle and become more self-aware. Colleagues discuss the benefits of student and teacher reflection, drawing on each other for expertise and support. All these things together result in a productive working environment for both teachers and students. Reflective practice helps educators make important, skillful decisions about how instruction will unfold each day. Reflection is not just an assessment tool—it is an essential habit for lifelong growth and success.

A Teacher's Take

Greg Moll's verdict on reflection? It's "real-life stuff." Here, he explains why, amid all the practices routinely recommended to teachers, "*This* is the thing you want to do and try."

We encourage you to begin this journey both for yourself and for your students. Take some time to reflect on what you value and believe about how reflective practices can help all students be more successful. Above all else, remain flexible, patient, and confident. Try some of the protocols in this book (more than once!), and give students lots of positive feedback as they hone their reflective skills. Explore the full descriptions of the protocols in the appendices. Of course, we hope you will carve out time for your own personal and professional reflection, too. Let's encourage our students to be curious, to wonder, and to see themselves as lifelong learners through the artful practice of reflection. We wish you success and joy on your journey!

Acknowledgments

Our work on reflection was shaped by learning alongside teachers, students, administrators, and conference presenters across the country. Classroom experiences and conversations informed the thinking that anchors this book, showing how intentional pauses for reflection, goal setting, and student ownership can be woven into daily learning. Family, supportive colleagues, and dear friends have been our cheerleaders throughout, encouraging us as we observed, listened, and reflected.

The Boyertown Area School District helped make this book possible by supporting the work of reflection. We are deeply grateful to Ursula Gamler, 4th grade ELA teacher; Greg Moll, 4th grade math/content teacher; and Kristen Sekkes, 4th grade math/content teacher, at Gilbertsville Elementary School, who welcomed us into their classrooms to observe and implement reflection protocols within daily instruction. Greg and Ursula also generously gave their time to engage in ongoing reflection with Catherine, trying protocols, processing what reflection could offer students, and providing thoughtful feedback. Their willingness to examine their own practice is featured throughout this book. We also extend our sincere thanks to Stephanie Petri, former principal of Gilbertsville Elementary School; Stephanie Landis, former director of teaching and learning, and Superintendent Scott Davidheiser, whose continued interest and encouragement sustained this reflection work over time.

Sincere thanks to teacher Jennifer Wyland, a dynamic and amazing middle school science teacher at Kutztown Area Middle School in Kutztown Area School District, who challenged her 7th graders to think deeply and creatively to make a difference both locally and globally. Thanks also to Upper Moreland Township School District for graciously supporting our work. Kolleen Bell, kindergarten teacher at Upper Moreland Primary School, and Kevin Black, 5th grade teacher (formerly 3rd grade), welcomed Lynne into their classrooms, and the intentional ways they make thinking visible and support reflection as a meaningful part of everyday learning are woven into this book. We thank Upper Moreland Principal Michael Bair, Assistant Principal Karen Rhoads, and Principal Dena Criss for a warm welcome. We also thank Superintendent Susan Elliott, Assistant Superintendent Larry Cannon, and Kelly Gallagher (Upper Moreland's federal program coordinator) for their unwavering support.

We also extend sincere thanks to the faculty and students at The Janus School in Mount Joy, Pennsylvania, who generously shared with us their work and thoughts on reflective practices. By allowing us to videotape their responses for the readers of this book, they helped us bring to life authentic teacher and student perspectives on the value of reflection. The Janus School is committed to serving diverse learners, and the window on the dynamic practices of its students and staff was invaluable.

Thank you to Ralph Abbott, whose expertise shooting and editing video allowed us to provide the videos we link to in this book.

We are deeply grateful to our editorial and publishing team. Thank you to our dear friend and editor, Bill Varner, who has been with us since the beginning of this journey. Bill, your belief in us, thoughtful guidance, and wisdom helped us grow as writers, imagine the possibilities, and shape this book into a finished product of which we are proud. Katie Martin, thank you for your guidance, responsiveness, and warmth throughout the editing and production process. You patiently responded to every question in a timely manner and helped us make important decisions. We thank everyone in our ISTE+ASCD Books family for their support and mentorship, including Jennifer Morgan, our frontline copyeditor; Judi Connelly, designer; Valerie Younkin, senior production designer; Christopher Logan, production manager; and Shajuan Martin, e-publishing specialist. Thanks also to proofreaders Laura Larson and Ruth Calkins, indexer Cynthia Landeen, and emergency substitute typesetter Cynthia Stock. Finally, a special shoutout to Cris Tovani for the time she gave to reviewing our manuscript and writing the Foreword.

From Lynne

I was fortunate to have three amazing coauthors, Catherine, Pérsida, and Aileen—all incredible educators who were willing to commit to our collaboration on this project. A special thanks to dear friends Teresa Lombardi and Jessica Kilcollum, who have always been my cheerleaders. Thank you to Dr. Pauline Schmidt and my West Chester Writing Project friends. I continue to grow as a reader, writer, and thinker because of your mentorship and leadership. A big thank-you to my husband, Ralph; my sister, Diane, and my brother-in-law, Willie; my goddaughters, Alex, Brooke, and Cait; and my two Welsh Corgis, Arthur and Rosie. Your love keeps me moving forward. Amid all the rest, love is all you need!

From Catherine

With deep appreciation, I acknowledge my coauthors, Lynne, Pérsida, and Aileen. Each contributed their distinct creative thinking, careful attention to detail, and deep classroom wisdom, shaping the book in meaningful ways. I am better for having learned alongside you.

I am endlessly grateful to my family—Margaret, Drew, John, Sarah, Sofia, Joey, and Timothy—whose encouragement nourished my spirit throughout this work. I am especially grateful to my husband, Steve, who spent countless hours processing ideas and thinking alongside me, offering steady support and a thoughtful perspective at every stage. A word of gratitude to my mentor and friend, Lynne Dorfman, for inviting me into the rewarding work of reflection, and to Bill Varner, who helped me gain my writing "sea legs" and encouraged me to trust myself. Finally, a special thank-you to my granddaughter, Sofia, whose curiosity and wonder continually remind me of the joy and discovery that reflection can bring.

From Pérsida

I am deeply honored to join three extraordinary colleagues in this important work. Lynne, Catherine, and Aileen, thank you for your profound insights, which have challenged and inspired me throughout our work together. I am also grateful to my husband, Bill. From the very beginning, what drew me to Bill was his sense of humor and the way he invited everyone into his circle. After more than three decades together, his kindness and compassion continue to inspire me to be a better, gentler human. I have been truly blessed to walk life's journey with him. And to my kids, Gabriela and Caleb: you and your dad are the best gifts in my life.

From Aileen

With deep gratitude to Lynne Dorfman, whose generosity, brilliance, and unwavering commitment to literacy continue to inspire both my teaching and my thinking. I am also continually amazed and grateful to call Pérsida Himmele not only a mentor I admire but also a colleague I am honored to learn alongside. My contributions to this book were held together by the love and patience of my husband, Michael, and our three remarkable children—Liam, River, and Meaza—who have supported every ambition, late night, and leap of faith along the way. *Dreams are not reached alone; they are built in the company of those who believe in them long before they come true.*

Appendixes

Appendix A: A Summary of Key Reflection Research

Suppose you were presented with the Nintendo Wii game *Karaoke Revolution: Glee* and asked to sing three songs as accurately as possible in volume, pitch, and note duration in exchange for 20 dollars. You spend 30 minutes singing the preselected songs—"Haven't Met You Yet" by Michael Bublé, "Don't You (Forget About Me)" by Simple Minds, and "I Will Survive" by Gloria Gaynor—as the lyrics appear across the screen. You are unaware that someone else is doing the same thing in another room. Unlike the person in the other room, after completing the first song, you are asked to spend five minutes reflecting on the experience: writing about what strategies you used to sing it and what you think you can do to be more effective in the task. After reflecting, you sing the next two songs. The person in the other room simply waits five minutes, without reflecting, before moving on. At the end of each song, the game's voice recognition software rates your performance score from 0 to 100. Who do you predict will get the higher score, you or the singer in the other room?

This was a scenario from a five-part study described in the research paper *Learning by Thinking: How Reflection Can Spur Progress Along the Learning Curve* by Giada Di Stefano of Bocconi University in Milan, Italy; Francesca Gino, independent; Gary Pisano, of Harvard University; and Bradley Staats, of the University of North Carolina (2023). In the study, of the 109 participants recruited from universities in the southeastern United States, participants who took part in reflection (the treatment group) sang more accurately, with an average of 41.85 percent accuracy, compared with the control group's 30.00 percent accuracy. The researchers concluded that the treatment group outperformed those who did not reflect.

In another fascinating part of the study, after completing a practice round, 256 participants executed rounds of five math puzzles each. They were given 20 seconds per puzzle. Upon completion of the first round, they were told whether their answers were correct and given a choice: spend three minutes thinking and writing about the strategies they used in the first round *or* spend three minutes practicing on another set of puzzles. More than 80 percent of the participants (210 out of 256) chose to practice for the additional three minutes, while the remaining 46 chose to reflect on the experience they accumulated in the first round. The results? The reflection group once again outperformed the control group. This finding doesn't discount the need for practice but rather highlights the value of reflection during the thinking and learning process.

The research continued in a field study experiment at a large business-process outsourcing firm that routinely puts new hires through intensive training. For this study, the control group went through the company's traditional two-week, all-day training while the study group went through the same training but was asked to reflect for 15 minutes at the close of each daily session. The first 10 minutes were dedicated to writing about the lessons they learned. Specifically, they were asked to write about at least two key lessons as specifically as possible. They were then given five minutes to explain their choices to another participant in the study group. At the end of the two weeks, both groups took the same final exam on all the information learned during training. The results were significant. The control group scored an average of 54.4 percent on the final exam, while the reflection group scored an average of 71.5 percent—a 17 percent boost in performance. Di Stefano and her group took their research one step further and tracked the same two groups in the first month on the job by checking customer satisfaction scores. The control group scored 77 percent, and the reflection group scored 91 percent. This discrepancy indicates reflection not only improved participants' original final exam scores but also had a "spillover" effect on their job.

The research supports the use of reflection to powerfully increase learners' overall performance, especially when building on foundational knowledge.

WORKSHEET

Appendix B: The Magnifying Glass Reflection Protocol

Reflection as a Magnifying Glass

Pausing to reflect as we're learning something new is like looking through a magnifying glass. We can zoom in to notice small details and complexities of the experience and then pull back to understand the bigger picture. This process helps us make meaning from what we're learning so that it sticks with us and doesn't slip away.

Instructions Name three things in your learning that are difficult, confusing, or a roadblock in your learning right now. Use these sentence starters if you need help: • I am stuck on . . . • I can't figure out . . . • My thinking is tangled up with . . .	Which problem did you star? ____________________ Reflect on this problem by answering the questions below: 1. Describe the learning experience.
1.	2. For this learning experience, what is going well or makes the most sense to you?
2.	3. What doesn't make sense? Where is your thinking tangled? How do you feel about it?
3. Place a star (★) next to the most challenging one and reflect in the box on the right.	4. What plan will you make to untangle your thinking so you can understand and move forward? Will you get help from a peer? Will you look for examples? Will you find a tutorial? Or will you find a different solution?
	Now that you have reflected on your learning experience, return to your problem and work through the hard parts. When you are finished, record what you did and how well it worked on the back of this sheet.

Appendix C: Brain Myths and Why Reflection Matters

Reflection is deeply connected to how our brains are wired. Share these five myths and truths with students to communicate to them how reflection plays an essential role in how the brain learns.

Myth #1: We only use 10 percent of our brains when we learn.

In reality...

All parts of the brain are in use at different times. It was once believed that only a small percentage of the brain was involved in the learning process, but advances in neuroscience research reveal that our brains experience a great deal of activity we were previously unaware of—even when we are at rest (Boyd, 2015; Hughes et al., 2013).

Reflection matters because...

When we are purposeful about reflection, many different hemispheres of our brains simultaneously "light up" (show activity on brain imagery). For example, the hippocampus connects new learning to what's stored in our memory, and the prefrontal cortex activates when we make decisions, plan, and set goals (Willis, 2020). What's even more amazing is that researchers now know that our brains remain active even when daydreaming or not thinking about a specific task, thanks to the default mode network. When we pause to reflect and let our minds wander, this network helps our brains learn—even when we may not be aware of it.

Myth #2: We each have a certain learning style with which our brains learn best.

In reality...

All learners use a variety of learning styles to make sense of information. The field of education has shifted away from its long-standing emphasis on students knowing their learning style and seeking out targeted instruction (i.e., believing that so-called visual learners must use images, charts, or diagrams, while auditory learners learn best by listening to lectures or podcasts and kinesthetic learners require hands-on experiences). Researchers now know that all learners benefit from applying all learning styles at various points, depending on the experience (Yale University Poorvu Center for Teaching and Learning, n.d.).

Reflection matters because...

Students strengthen their self-awareness by figuring out which strategies and learning styles work best for them in which situations. They needn't limit their learning to one style; instead, they should work toward becoming more flexible learners (Di Stefano et al., 2023). Explain that their prefrontal cortex functions like a symphony conductor does, activating many different lobes in the brain to work together, regardless of what's being learned and how.

Myth #3: Some people are just smart and good at learning, so if you're not, you may as well give up.

In reality...

The brain and its ability to learn are not fixed. In fact, the human brain is pliable or moldable, a property called *neuroplasticity*. With 100 billion neuron cells sending electrical impulses that result in quadrillions of neural connections, the brain has an amazing capacity to grow and reorganize itself (Carey, 2015; Siegel & Bryson, 2012). As a matter of fact, research shows that increased difficulty and struggle during practice leads to more learning and greater structural change in the brain (Boyd, 2015). To retain skills or information, the brain requires a great deal of practice and repetition to add new cells and literally change its makeup.

Reflection matters because...

As an intentional pause that allows us to revisit new information and strengthen neural pathways, reflection makes learning stick. It also gives us hope and confidence that we can learn the things we want to learn, not only when the learning feels successful or rewarding but also when we feel stuck in failure patterns (Willis, 2020). When given space for reflection, we notice what we could not see before, such as patterns in our thought processes or behaviors and strategies that worked well for us. We have a chance to untangle our missteps, and this allows us to turn our learning experience into new and valuable insights and knowledge. Reflection provides a way to move forward in our learning. It can lead to "aha" moments that fuel confidence and joy in the learning process.

Myth #4: I get it today, so now I know it for good.

In reality...

Memorizing new content or skills or "getting it" during a lesson doesn't mean we've truly learned something. The brain has both short-term and long-term memory. Short-term memory learning results from a rapid increase in chemical concentrations in the brain as it takes in new information, allowing us to hold on to information temporarily. When a learning experience is coming to an end, the brain must decide whether to retain the new information or let it fade away (Sousa, 2023). This explains why we think we understand a science concept one day, only to forget it the next. To make learning last, we need to put in effort to move it from short-term to long-term memory.

Reflection matters because...

Reflection—asking questions such as *What did I learn? What does it matter? How does it connect to what I already know?*—plays an important role in enhancing long-term memory. When we reflect, we activate parts of our brain that help us think more deeply (i.e., we engage in higher-order thinking), which is the kind of thinking that takes us to deeper, longer-lasting learning. Long-term memory storage takes more time because the brain physically changes in size and shape during the process (Di Stefano et al., 2023; Siegel & Drulis, 2023; Willis, 2006).

Myth #5: Making mistakes is the same as failure.

In reality...

We need to make mistakes because that's how we learn. The moment we realize we've erred, our brain lights up and begins the search to figure out why. The brain is very sensitive to mistakes and will adjust and respond more slowly with a next attempt (Sousa, 2023). As we make adjustments to our learning, our brains' circuitry adapts, making new connections. When we make mistakes, it's important to press pause on self-doubt and judgment (Ellis et al., 2014). Instead of feeling embarrassed or discouraged, we should reframe our thinking, saying to ourselves, *This is a learning zone* or *productive struggle is necessary.*

Reflection matters because...

It helps us work through failure by asking ourselves, *What worked? What didn't work? Where am I going wrong? How can I figure this out?* When we reflect, we invite new possibilities and strengthen the prefrontal cortex, which supports decision-making and problem-solving capacity. We also apply metacognitive thinking skills by becoming aware of which strategies worked for us and which did not. If we don't embrace failure, our learning slows, and we miss the opportunity to grow beyond thinking that is comfortable to us. Failure can teach us how to be resilient—if we let it.

Appendix D: The Question Formation Technique (QFT) Protocol

The eight-step Question Formation Technique (QFT) Protocol (see Rothstein & Santana, 2011; Right Question Institute, n.d.) guides students in generating questions based on a focus (e.g., a book, a movie, an experiment, or other stimuli). As students formulate questions, they not only actively engage with the content but also take ownership of their learning and practice critical thinking. The QFT protocol has its roots in a high school dropout prevention program developed in a small Massachusetts community in the 1980s. Social workers for the program realized that parents of underserved students were hesitant to attend school meetings because they didn't know what questions to ask. Engaging parents in training to learn to formulate questions resulted in a sharp increase in participation in school meetings. Subsequently, the practice was adapted to professional and educational settings.

Used in the classroom, the protocol trains students to use higher-order thinking to craft questions. Benefits of the technique include higher, deeper student engagement; greater understanding of content; and increased knowledge retention. Additionally, students develop a sense of inclusivity and community as they take on responsibility for the direction of their learning. The protocol is a good fit for book clubs, debate preparation, or getting ready to participate in Socratic circles.

Instructions

To start, have participants sit in groups of three or four. Provide each group with a blank sheet of paper and markers. Regular copy paper will work, but a large sheet of paper (e.g., 12" x 18") allows everyone in the group to see and participate more easily. Prepare your Question Focus (QFocus; see Step 1). It can be a book that participants have already read, a nonfiction passage, a video, or a topic or concern you wish to research and discuss. Facilitators may choose to invite participants to contribute ideas for the focus ahead of time. The only rule is that the focus should never be a question. Plan for enough time for the process, which usually takes about four to eight minutes per step.

Authors' Note: This version of the protocol includes supports created by Catherine Gehman to better guide students toward deeper thinking and a higher level of discussion.

Step 1 Design the QFocus and prepare	1. Design the QFocus. It should meet the following criteria: a. Concise b. Narrow in scope c. Objective (does not reflect facilitator's bias or perspective) d. In the form of a statement (i.e., not a question) e. Related to intended learning outcomes f. Encourages an exploration of multiple ideas and possibilities 2. Introduce the QFT model and explain the process. 3. Communicate the focus to participants and post it for reference. 4. Ask students to sit in groups of three to four. 5. Provide large paper and pens/markers to each group. 6. Ask students to choose a scribe. EXAMPLE *Today, I will share a simple process that will help you generate a high volume of well-thought-out questions based on the book we read in class. Instead of me giving you a list of questions to discuss, YOU will come up with questions based on these rules:* *1. Ask as many questions as come to mind.* *2. Do not pause to answer, judge, or discuss the questions.* *3. Do not revise the questions. The scribe should write them down exactly as stated.* *4. When someone makes a statement, turn it into a question.*
Step 2 Discuss (2 mins.)	1. Give participants time to discuss the following questions: a. What might be difficult about applying the rules? b. Which rule poses the most difficulty for you? Why? 2. State the focus, resisting the urge to explain it. EXAMPLE *Your focus for today is "On the Sidewalk Bleeding" by American author Evan Hunter.*
Step 3 Formulate questions (4–5 mins.)	1. Instruct participants to generate as many questions as possible in the allotted time. 2. Support struggling participants by directing them to think about a keyword or two in the QFocus. You may ask them questions related to those words to get them thinking. 3. Avoid providing questions yourself.
Step 4 Distinguish between open-ended and closed questions (5 mins.)	1. Explain closed and open-ended questions to students: a. Closed questions can be answered with *yes*, *no*, or a one-word response. Often, closed questions begin with *is*, *does*, *can*, or *are*. b. Open-ended questions require an explanation. They often begin with *why*, *how*, or *what*. 2. Ask participants to categorize each of their questions by marking them with a *C* (closed) or an *O* (open-ended). 3. Ask the following questions, giving enough time for participants to respond to each: a. What are some advantages of closed questions? b. What are some disadvantages? c. What are some advantages of open-ended questions? d. What are some disadvantages?

Step 5 Rework and improve the questions (4 mins.)	1. Guide participants in making changes to their list of questions. 2. Change one closed question to an open-ended question. 3. Change one open-ended question to a closed question.
Step 6 Prioritize questions (4 mins.)	1. Instruct participants to review their questions. 2. Ask them to place a star next to the three most important questions, keeping the QFocus in mind. *Note:* You may want to change your prioritization instructions to target a certain emphasis. For example, you may want students to think about what questions they need answers to first, or what questions they want to ask of a particular person.
Step 6A (Optional) Create an action plan	1. Ask participants the following questions: a. What will you do with the priority questions? b. What information would you like to gather with these questions? c. How will you go about getting that information?
Step 7 Share the work (5 mins.)	1. Ask each group to share their list of questions with another group or with the entire group. 2. Guide students' discussion with the following questions: a. What questions did your group change from open-ended to closed? b. Why did you choose your three priority questions? c. Did you create an action plan (optional step)?
Step 8 Reflect (4–5 mins.)	1. Ask participants to think and write about what they learned, using the following prompts: a. What did you learn from this activity? b. How can you move your learning forward with what you learned?

Appendix E: The Sticky Note Reflection Pathway Protocol

The Sticky Note Reflection Pathway Protocol is an effective way to support struggling students to move beyond surface-level ideas. It works especially well with videos, fiction passages, nonfiction articles, and more. It is best used with individuals or small groups to help them strengthen their initial thinking and to stimulate meaningful conversation.

Students use a structured map to expand a simple thought into deeper, evidence-supported reflection.

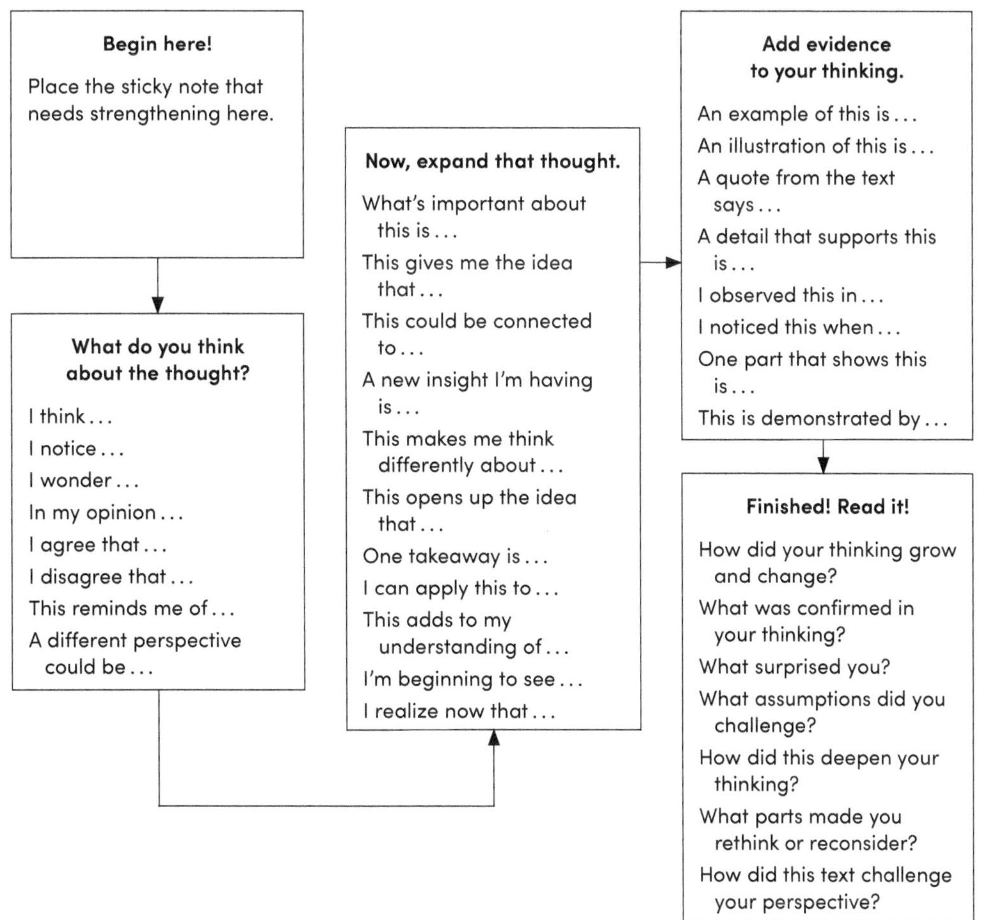

Preparation

Before you work through the steps of the protocol, consider posting sentence stems such as the following to provide students with extra support as they work to expand their thinking.

- I think we are studying this unit because...
- Something in the lesson that surprised me was...
- Something that puzzled or perplexed me was...
- What I understand is... but I don't get...
- Emotions I am feeling about the lesson are...
- What worked in my learning today was...
- What didn't work for me was...
- I used my time well for...
- I didn't use my time well during...
- After I checked my work again, I discovered that...
- My effort today was...
- These sketches and drawings show my learning...
- Goals I have for the next lesson are...
- After learning..., I would like to create a project...
- I'm going to need this in my life because...
- The important thing about this is...
- As I say this, I am realizing that...
- This is giving me the idea that...
- An example of this is...
- This shows...
- Another example of this is...
- This connects to...
- I see that...
- The thought I have about this is...
- To add on... (Additionally...; Furthermore...)
- The reason for this is.... Another reason is...
- This is important because...
- On the other hand...
- This is similar to...
- This is different because... (In contrast to this...)

Instructions

When students are first learning this technique, the teacher should model the process for them. After a few rounds, students should be able to facilitate the steps on their own. Practice the Sticky Note Reflection Pathway Protocol after watching a documentary, reading a story, working through a science lab, or analyzing a primary source. Use the protocol to build students' confidence and skill with metacognitive thinking and academic conversation, and encourage them to move toward independent reflection without using the scaffold of the form over time.

Step 1 Prepare	Have students sit in groups of three to five. Distribute materials to each student: Sticky Note Reflection Pathway form; three 3" x 3" sticky notes (have more ready for later if needed); a lined 5" x 7" sticky note; and the video, passage, or article for reflection. EXAMPLE *Please sit in groups of three to five. Each of you should have three small sticky notes, one large lined sticky note, a Sticky Note Reflection Pathway form, and a copy of the article we're discussing.*
Step 2 Read or view material	After reading or viewing the selected material, ask each student to write one thought or question per sticky note (one sentence is sufficient). EXAMPLE *Place your small sticky notes in front of you and be ready to record your thinking following the video. You can write a complete thought, a simple statement, a word, or a question.*
Step 3 Share	Students take turns sharing what they wrote. EXAMPLE *Take two to three minutes to share your thoughts with your group. Each person should have an opportunity to speak.*
Step 4 Choose a thought or question to strengthen	Ask students to review their three sticky notes and select the "weakest" one, allowing them to interpret what "weakest" means (e.g., shortest, least developed). EXAMPLE *Now that you've shared your sticky notes, let's focus on one that needs some growth. Find the sticky note that feels the least developed. Maybe it's too short, a bit too general, or something you don't fully understand yet. This is the one we're going to work with.*
Step 5 Begin the Sticky Note Reflection Pathway	Have students place their weakest sticky note in the box labeled "Begin here!" on the Sticky Note Reflection Pathway. EXAMPLE *Place your weakest sticky note on the Sticky Note Reflection Pathway in the box labeled "Begin here!" You are going to take your sticky note on a reflection journey that will strengthen, deepen, and expand your thinking.*
Step 6 Go deeper	Guide students through expanding their thinking using the provided sentence stems at each step on the Sticky Note Reflection Pathway: EXAMPLE *Take a moment to think about what you wrote. What do you mean? Dive into the idea behind it. Ask yourself,* What's the heart of this thought? Why does it matter? *This is where we start to add more details and build on your original thought.*

Step 7 Stretch	Have students expand on their thoughts. EXAMPLE *Once you've clarified what you mean, it's time to stretch that thought even bigger! How can we make this idea broader? What else connects to it? Think about other examples, perspectives, or things you've seen, read, or heard that can help expand this thought.*
Step 8 Provide evidence	Guide students to add evidence to their thought. EXAMPLE *Now that you've stretched your idea, let's take it to the next level. What evidence or examples can you add to strengthen this thinking? It could be a personal experience, a fact from the material we just read, or even a quote. What real-world connection can you use to support your thought?*
Step 9 Transfer	For the final step, ask students to transfer their expanded thinking onto the large lined sticky note. EXAMPLE *Once you've added the evidence, write your expanded idea on your lined sticky note. This is your final reflection. When you're ready, we'll share and discuss how your thinking has changed or deepened.*
Step 10 Engage in deeper discussion	Have small groups reconvene to share and discuss their final reflections. EXAMPLE *As you discuss your thoughts with your group, share how your thinking changed. Allow for new ideas to emerge during this discussion. How did your thoughts or questions change or deepen as a result of this activity?*

Future Possibilities

- First, model the process. Then, after a few rounds, have students facilitate the steps.
- Practice the Sticky Note Reflection Pathway Protocol after watching a documentary, reading a story, working through a science lab, or analyzing a primary source.
- Encourage students to move toward independent reflection without using the scaffold of the form over time.
- Use the protocol to build students' confidence and skill with metacognitive thinking and academic conversation.

Appendix F: The Neuro-Reflection Protocol

The Neuro-Reflection Protocol is a six-step process that supports students in reflecting on a learning experience. It begins with students using a Likert-like scale to rate their experience with a targeted skill or concept and the difficulty level of the learning. They then respond to four open-ended prompts, identifying what challenged them, what their strengths are, and a time their thinking was confused. Finally, they evaluate their growth. Reflecting in this way clears a pathway for learners to practice good academic habits and identify areas for improvement.

Instructions

The structure of the Neuro-Reflection Protocol helps students dive deeper into their learning experiences, yielding more meaningful analysis. While the reflective process does take a few more minutes than an exit ticket (for example), the results go deeper. When practiced frequently, students are more likely to remember and use the prompts themselves, making reflection an everyday habit.

The worksheet that follows takes approximately 15 minutes to complete. Consider using the protocol with small groups of struggling learners to help them work through obstacles while acknowledging the emotional component of the struggle. Once students are comfortable using the protocol, make copies of the form accessible to students for independent use.

Neuro-Reflection: Zooming In to Strengthen Learning

Name: ______________________ Date: ______________________

Subject: ______________________ Skill/Concept: ______________________

1. My experience with this skill/concept:

Brand new 1 2 3 4 5 I've done this many times

2. For me, doing or learning this felt:

Easy 1 2 3 4 5 Impossible

One brain muscle I built thanks to this lesson:	Thinking that was hard or got tangled up for me in this lesson and how I felt about it:
One thing I appreciate about how this lesson made me grow:	How knowing this skill or concept adds value to my life:

3. Did you gain an unexpected insight during this reflection process? If so, explain.

WORKSHEET

Protocol Steps

<table>
<tr><td>Step 1</td><td>Introduce the Neuro-Reflection Worksheet and provide each student with their own copy to fill out.

EXAMPLE
We're going to take a moment to reflect on our lesson on [skill/concept]. To begin, fill out the information at the top of the page. Next, I'll guide you through the prompts on the worksheet, which challenge you to think deeply about this learning experience.</td></tr>
<tr><td>Step 2</td><td>Guide students to rate the experience they have with the skill or concept and its level of difficulty.

Clarifying prompts:
• How is evaluating your experience with the skill or concept helpful to you?
• How does experience level affect how you feel about the learning experience?
• Why did you rate the difficulty level the way you did?
• Why is it important for you to connect your experience level to how difficult you think the skill or concept is?</td></tr>
<tr><td>Step 3
Vocabulary
challenge
cognition
connection
endurance
focus
grit
growth mindset
neuroplasticity
perseverance
reflection
resilience</td><td>Identify strengthened thinking.

EXAMPLE
Let's talk about "brain muscle." While your brain isn't actually a muscle, it can be strengthened similarly to the muscles in your body. When you run, lift weights, or exercise, your muscles get stronger and your body becomes more flexible and runs more efficiently. The same is true for your brain. When you exercise it by working hard to learn something new and thinking about it over and over, your brain's neurons are firing and making new connections. The scientific name for the brain's ability to change and grow in response to learning is neuroplasticity.
  With this in mind (no pun intended), just as physical exercise requires hard work, your brain needs positive messages. When you struggle with something, learn to say, I can do hard things or I'll get help or I won't give up. This is called a growth mindset—believing that instruction, practice, and hard work can help you make progress or change something.

Clarifying prompts:
Can you recall a moment during this lesson when you felt stuck? How did that make you feel? Were you able to overcome that challenge on your own or with help?
• I got stuck when ________, so I ________.
• My thinking got all tangled up at the point where ________, but now I see ________.
• I asked ________ for help, and then ________.</td></tr>
</table>

Step 4 **Vocabulary** challenge confront demanding difficult endure get by grapple handle rigorous struggle suffer survive tough wrestle	Evaluate learning obstacles. EXAMPLE *Sometimes, learning can be going smoothly, and then a roadblock appears out of nowhere. Or you feel like your clear thinking suddenly got tangled up. This happens to all of us, especially with new learning.* *What's important to understand is the value in working through obstacles and knots. We learn from the complications and the mistakes we make. You might try different ways to sort out what's holding you back on your own, but ask for help if you need to. No matter the situation, don't give up or pretend everything is OK. Instead, examine the situation and pinpoint where you feel stuck so you can work it out and move forward.* Clarifying prompts: What's one thing you appreciate about the progress you made? How did your efforts contribute to your learning? • I felt proud when I ________ because it showed my growth. • At first, I found it challenging to ________, but with effort, I was able to ________. • One achievement I'm proud of is ________ because it took a lot of practice. • When I think about my progress in ________, I remember how far I've come. • I realized that facing challenges like ________ helped me learn ________.
Step 5 **Vocabulary** accomplishment acknowledge appreciate celebrate empower enjoy enrich fulfillment gratitude insight milestone perseverance progression recognize reflection resilience tenacity transformation triumph welcome	Appreciate growth. EXAMPLE *Now, let's focus on appreciating the learning process as well as the growth you have made. Take a moment to notice what you've learned and the work you've done. Reflect on the effort and energy you put forth. Celebrate that progress!* *Acknowledging your achievements leads to increased motivation, higher self-esteem, and a sense of accomplishment. You will find that you want to continue to learn and push through challenges.* Clarifying prompts: • How does knowing this concept or skill add value to your life? • Now that I know ________, I use it to ________. • Understanding this concept has helped me ________. • This skill adds value because it allows me to ________. • I realize that applying what I've learned has inspired me to ________.

Step 6 **Vocabulary** application awareness contribution empowerment engagement impact innovation integration relevance transformation	Acknowledge lesson's value and personal application. EXAMPLE *Connecting what you learn to the real world is important because it helps you see the value of your knowledge and skills. When you understand how your learning affects your daily life, you become a more motivated and engaged learner. This can inspire you to take action and make positive changes—not just in your own life but also in your community and the world around you.* Clarifying prompts: • Think about your life. Imagine how this new learning can change your life. How will knowing this be important in your future? How could you use it to make the world a better place? • Now that I know _______, I can _______. • Understanding this concept has helped me to _______. • This skill adds value because it allows me to make a difference by _______. • What I've learned has inspired me to _______.
Wrap-Up	In a whole-class discussion, invite learners to share something that stands out to them from this reflection process. (Note: Participation should be voluntary to avoid requiring students to reveal personal or sensitive information.) EXAMPLE *Thank you for reflecting on your learning. Remember, taking time to think about our learning helps us grow and prepares us for future challenges. Your ability to reflect is a powerful tool!* *Now it's time to answer the final question on the worksheet: Did you gain an unexpected insight during this reflection process? Write your response on the back of the page.* *Once you've completed your responses, we'll come together as a class so that you may share any insights you've gained.* Clarifying prompts: • What stands out to you about this lesson? • How has your thinking changed? • How can you use this information to change your approach to learning?

Appendix G: The 5Rs Framework Reflection Protocol

The 5Rs framework (Bain et al., 2002) engages learners in five stages of reflection—report, respond, relating, reason, and reconstruct—to make sense of a learning experience. It's an effective way for them to restructure their thinking and process an experience through higher-order thinking. The focus of the reflection is entirely up to the learner; they may choose to focus on academics or a personal experience. The protocol can be guided by a facilitator or completed independently.

This model can be applied to academic, personal, or professional situations. Think about how you would revise the questions to fit the needs of your students and the experiences they are reflecting on.

Instructions

Step 1 Report the context or background of the experience	1. Briefly describe the experience, problem, or issue you are reflecting on. a. What happened? b. What are the key aspects of this experience? c. Who was involved? d. What set the experience into motion? 2. Include essential elements of the situation for context. a. What happened was . . . b. I noticed that . . . c. Someone else's point of view is . . . d. Establish the time frame (e.g., Yesterday, . . .; Last month, . . .). EXAMPLE *Yesterday, I met with my group to create a plan for our final project. We were given a rubric for guidelines. Although we got to work quickly, it took time to discuss what we want to do. Also, some in the group were distracted. We only have five class periods to complete the project, and I am concerned we won't have enough time to finish.*
Step 2 Respond by recording observations, feelings, thoughts, etc.	1. Describe your personal response to the experience, situation, or problem. a. What was I feeling before, during, and after? b. What did I think? c. What made me feel this way? 2. Include your feelings and thoughts about the experience. a. I felt . . . b. I thought . . . c. I was under the impression that . . . d. I believe . . . 3. Record your observations. 4. Write down any questions you may have.

Authors' note: This version of the protocol includes supports created by Catherine Gehman to guide students toward deeper thinking and a higher level of discussion.

Step 2—(*cont.*) Respond by recording observations, feelings, thoughts, etc.	EXAMPLE *I felt optimistic that we would be able to come up with a plan and assign tasks. I felt this way because we are all friends and we all get along. I hoped to take the lead, but someone else in the group decided to be the leader before I could volunteer. That person said we should start by looking at the rubric. I agreed. As we went through, there were a lot of sidebar conversations. I tried to keep it going by saying, "Hey, let's get back on track," but that didn't help. I left the classroom feeling frustrated because we wasted time. I was worried because we have a deadline.*
Step 3 Relate the experience to prior knowledge, skills, expertise, self-awareness, etc.	1. Describe your understanding of how the situation relates to your knowledge and past experiences. 2. Make a connection between your past experiences and what is currently happening. a. Have I seen this before? b. What is similar and different? c. What knowledge or skills do I have to contribute? d. What knowledge or skills don't I possess? e. Do I need to get advice or clarity from someone more experienced? f. This reminds me of . . . EXAMPLE *I'm an organized student and I care about doing projects well. In the past when I've worked in groups, I experienced similar things such as sidebar conversations or group members being distracted or off task. I don't know how to talk to my group without feeling afraid they will get upset with me. I don't know how to help us get back on track. I think I may need some help.*
Step 4 Reason through significant factors or theories to explain or support the experience	1. Explore the experience by elaborating on it in writing. Discuss significant contributing factors and how they are important to understanding the experience. a. What is the most important aspect about the situation? Why? b. Is there research, literature, or expert voices that I can consult to help bring clarity to the experience? c. How many others see this situation? d. How do different perspectives affect the way I see the experience? e. How would someone who is knowledgeable about these types of situations respond? f. I understand . . . g. ________ implies that . . . h. Evidence to support my idea is . . . i. One theory is . . .

Step 4—(*cont.*) Reason through significant factors or theories to explain or support the experience	EXAMPLE *I have been in groups before where the same problems have arisen—sidebar talking, lack of focus, no motivation. I figured it was because we just weren't a good match of personalities. For this group, however, we were able to choose who we wanted to work with. I was excited because we all get along well. I was surprised we didn't get anything done because I assumed a good match in personalities was the key. One theory I have as to why we couldn't get things moving is that maybe all the others feel like I do—afraid they may upset their friends if they speak up. Another thought is that they just might not care as much as I do. I need to talk to my teacher and explain the situation and ask for advice on how to work with this group but not get anyone in trouble.*
Step 5 Reconstruct your experience to plan future actions	1. Reframe or reconstruct the experience by drawing conclusions from the four previous steps. 2. Develop an action plan that includes ideas for what to do next and form an argument for why it will work. 3. Evaluate how your understanding deepened through this reflection journey. 4. Include the literature, expertise, and advice you referred to during the Relate and Reason stages. 5. Describe your plan to move forward. a. What do I need to do differently in the future? b. What might work? Why? c. What might not work? Why? d. Are there different options I have not previously thought of? e. Are my ideas supported by theory? f. What changes can I make to benefit others? g. What might happen if . . .? h. I learned that . . . i. Moving forward, I will . . . j. Next time, I could . . . k. I may consider . . . EXAMPLE *As I reflect on this entire experience, I see that when things became difficult, I became quiet. I realize now that the sidebar conversations may be a sign that others are also confused. Next time, I will take this as an opportunity to lean in rather than pull back. I plan to express that I want to move forward together and not on my own and not worry so much about negative responses. Next time, I could ask the question "What do you all think is the best way to approach this project?"*

Appendix H: The What? So What? Now What? Protocol

The What? So What? Now What? protocol (Borton, 1970) helps a student derive meaning from an experience and explore how to move forward by posing three questions:

- **What?**—Describe the experience by explaining the context, facts, and feelings involved.
- **So What?**—Find meaning by thinking about theories to help make sense of the experience.
- **Now What?**—Focus on creating an action plan for the future based on responses to the previous questions.

The example below centers on a teacher's experience of leading a small-group project in the classroom.

Instructions

As you guide participants through the reflective process, encourage them to be honest and maintain an open, nonjudgmental attitude. Remind them that reflection leads to a greater ability to unlock creativity and possible solutions to existing problems. The protocol can be applied to academic, personal, or professional situations, with the questions tailored to fit the needs of participants.

Step 1 What? Describe the experience	Look as objectively as you can at the experience. Avoid dwelling on feelings and focus on facts and details. Key questions: • What happened? • Who was involved? • When did it happen? • Where did it happen? • Why did this happen? • How did it happen? EXAMPLE *On Monday, in science class, students worked in small groups to complete a design challenge: build a bridge using straws and tape. Four groups completed the challenge, but one group did not; those students left feeling frustrated. I was surprised because I thought that group would collaborate well. The activity was intended to promote teamwork as well as engineering principles. The group could not complete the activity because they disagreed about the design plan. Instead of coming up with one idea and working on it together, they split up the materials and built two different designs. They then ran out of time.*

Authors' note: This version of the protocol includes supports created by Catherine Gehman to guide students toward deeper thinking and a higher level of discussion.

Step 2 So what? Understand the experience	Interpret the experience by analyzing how you and others feel about it. Explore without blaming or judging yourself or others. Key questions: • How did I feel about the experience? • Did something trigger an emotional response? What was it? • What was puzzling or confusing to me? • What was going through my mind at the time? • What did I learn as a result? • What does this show me about the way I work? • What could I have done differently? • What would I do the same? • How did this affect my relationship with others, if at all? • What information, theories, or expert voices could be helpful to me? EXAMPLE *I was frustrated with the students because the instructions were clear, and we had set expectations for group work the previous day. I purposely did not intervene while class was in session. Instead, I observed and took notes. I was puzzled that the student who usually takes a leadership role sat back and was quiet. Later, I became aware that this student was frustrated and overwhelmed, and subsequently shut down. I realize now that I could have supported all the groups better with printed-out sentence stems and a final reflection. It's a good reminder that collaboration skills need to be scaffolded.*
Step 3 Now what? Create a plan to move forward	Key questions: • What steps can I take for improvement? • How can I move forward in a way that ensures success? • What changes do I need to make in my attitude? • What should I take into account as I make the changes? • How can I prevent a problem in the future? • What worked that I should repeat? EXAMPLE *I made a plan to model collaboration skills once again. I'll have students model using sentence stems and ask another teacher for advice on how to communicate students' roles in group work to them. What worked was that I observed and kept detailed notes, which gave me important insights. I also gave students space to work out their issues, but I learned that when a group is struggling, I may need to intervene more.*

Appendix I: Expressive Writing Versus Reflective Writing

Expressive Writing

First, and foremost, expressive writing is personal writing. The writer shares thoughts, ideas, feelings, and questions about his or her experiences. Usually written in first-person point of view, it exhibits the author's voice. The author tells the reader how he or she feels.

Reflective Writing

Though also personal, reflective writing often moves beyond recounting an experience and into an exploration of how that particular experience has shaped the writer. The goal of reflective writing is not to share final thoughts on a topic; on the contrary, it is a vehicle for exploring and discovering new thoughts. In reflective writing, the author often looks at the past as a means of looking at the future. (Gallagher, 2011, p. 25)

The following examples illustrate the differences between expressive and reflective writing for English language arts, math, and history:

Subject Area	Expressive Writing	Reflective Writing
English language arts	I was so nervous when Annemarie took the basket that had the envelope tucked under her uncle's lunch. We were all sitting on the edge of our seats, wondering if she was going to get taken by the German soldiers who stopped her and fed the bread to their dogs. Annemarie was brave and thought on her feet.	When we read *Number the Stars* by Lois Lowry today, I thought about courage as I read the part where her mother tells her to bring a basket with bread and cheese to her uncle and to put the important envelope underneath it. As I read how she was stopped by the German soldiers, I wondered what I would do if I were Annemarie. Would I be that brave? Would I be able to think on my feet like she did? I just don't know. What I do know is that I want to be like her. It reminds me of something my teacher told us. She said that being brave doesn't mean we're not afraid. It means we do what we have to do, knowing we can't control the outcome. She told us that there's always a little fear in every courageous act.

Subject Area	Expressive Writing	Reflective Writing
Math	I was super-frustrated and kind of embarrassed in math today. I got how to move variables to one side but forgot how to add variables. My teacher tried to help me when he saw I was really lost, but he did it on the board and I got it wrong in front of everyone. I hate math.	In math today, we learned how to solve equations with variables on both sides. My teacher showed us how to balance both sides of the equation by using inverse operations. I kept forgetting to switch the sign when I subtracted a negative number, but I remembered how my teacher says we have to persevere and not quit. The cool thing is that I'm starting to remember how to do these equations without relying on my teacher as much.
History	I felt sad to learn about Japanese-American internment camps in class today. It's so sad to think that good people were forced to leave their homes and live in camps with barbed wire and guards just because they were Japanese. I had no idea this happened during WWII.	I felt a wide range of emotions when I learned about Japanese-American internment camps in class today. There was so much fear and suspicion after the bombing of Pearl Harbor. This led to Executive Order 9066. My teacher explained that the West Coast became a military exclusion zone, and that meant all people of Japanese heritage were forced out of their homes and had to live in guarded military camps for almost three years. Also, there wasn't any real evidence that these people were spies or had done anything bad. How could this have happened? Wasn't there a better way to deal with all of this? It reminds me of the mass deportations of immigrants I'm reading about in the news. It's easy to remove myself from these things that happened in history when I read it from a book, but when I think about the fact that these were and are real people with families, livelihoods, and lives they want to live, I don't even know how to wrap my head around it. I've decided to take some books out of the library to learn more about this time in history.

Appendix J: The Compass Protocol

Reflection means pausing on purpose to work through learning that perplexed, puzzled, or surprised us. We think about what was difficult or easy, and we embrace our failures and successes so that we can learn from those experiences. It's like using a compass to guide our learning: We orient ourselves by thinking about where we have been, where we are now, and how we will navigate to a new place in our learning.

Take a few minutes to think back on your learning in the unit we just completed. Go through the descriptions listed on the Challenges and Strengths Checklists. For each area, mark if it was a challenge or a strength for you; check the third column if this description didn't apply to the unit. Then complete the rating scales.

Unit: ____

1. How this unit went for me:

Not well 1 2 3 4 5 Very well

2. The level of effort I put in:

Did not try or care 1 2 3 4 5 Worked as hard as I could

3. The level of perseverance I had:

Gave up easily 1 2 3 4 5 Didn't give up even when it was hard

4. The level of precision I used:

Didn't care about precision 1 2 3 4 5 Cared about and checked my work

Pause for a moment to read over your ratings and think about the unit. What worked for you? What didn't work for you? Share your thinking with a partner, and answer the questions below.

WORKSHEET

WORKSHEET

1. Reflect on the unit.

a. What was confusing or difficult?

b. What barriers or roadblocks got in the way of your learning? Give an example.

c. How can you be more successful in the future? Be specific.

2. Reflect on the strengths you demonstrated in the unit.

a. What went well?

b. Why did it go well?

c. What attitudes, actions, and strengths contributed to your success? Give an example.

d. How can you repeat these strengths in the next unit? Be specific.

3. What is the next unit you will study?

a. What changes do you need to make to be successful?

b. How can you repeat actions that were successful in the past?

c. What level of effort will you put in? How will you persevere?

d. What else comes to mind? Create one or more goals for yourself.

Sketch or draw yourself meeting your goal(s) in the next unit.

Appendix K: Challenges and Strengths Checklists by Subject Area

As students review each quality and consider how they interact with the unit they are reflecting on, ask them to place a check in one of the three columns.

Challenges and Strengths Checklist: Math

Quality	This area is a challenge for me.	This area is a strength for me.	This area doesn't apply to me.
Anxiety—How I handle uncomfortable feelings about struggles with math			
Attitude—My confidence, enjoyment, and motivation in math class			
Preparedness—My ability to have all my supplies and everything I need ready for class and to do my homework on time			
Vocabulary load—How I handle big math words			
Computational skills/math facts—How I get to the exact answer			
Working memory—My ability to hold information in my head while I do another part of the process			
Understanding the problem—How I process what's being asked and know what I have to do			
Visual representations—How I use reading, drawing, and writing to understand the problem (e.g., using a number line, drawing a graph to represent an equation)			
Spatial imagery—How I understand and manipulate objects (e.g., objects positioned in a 2D or 3D space, rotating or flipping objects)			
Proofreading—My ability to go back over all the steps and check for mistakes			
Stamina/perseverance—How I stay with the problem and don't quit			
Focus—How I concentrate on the task I am doing			
Growth mindset—My ability to embrace challenges and mistakes as a path to success			

WORKSHEET

Challenges and Strengths Checklist: Math—(*continued*)

Quality	This area is a challenge for me.	This area is a strength for me.	This area doesn't apply to me.
Math strategies—How I use strategies I've acquired in class (e.g., visualizing, drawing, labeling, rereading, highlighting, underlining, giving the final answer)			
Resources—How I use textbooks, manipulatives, online resources, anchor charts, or a reflection journal to support my thinking			
Seeking help—My ability to self-advocate by asking questions or getting clarification for what I don't understand			

Challenges and Strengths Checklist: Social Studies

Quality	This area is a challenge for me.	This area is a strength for me.	This area doesn't apply to me.
Anxiety—How I handle uncomfortable feelings about struggles with social studies/history			
Attitude—My confidence, enjoyment, and motivation in social studies/history class			
Preparedness—My ability to have all my supplies and everything I need ready for class and to do my homework on time			
Vocabulary load—How I handle social studies concepts and Tier 3 vocabulary for future use, including names of people, places, events, and primary source documents			
Evaluating—My ability to critically examine an author's purposes, point of view, and arguments			
Working memory—My ability to hold information in my head while I do another part of the process			
Understanding the task—How I process what's being asked and know what I have to do			
Visual representations—How I use graphs, maps, diagrams, infographics, timelines, and data charts to gain deeper understanding of the readings			

Quality	This area is a challenge for me.	This area is a strength for me.	This area doesn't apply to me.
Thinking like a historian—How I use cause/effect relationships, chronology of events, and a problem/solution framework to understand how the past influences present and future life and the world			
Proofreading—My ability to go back over all the steps and check for mistakes			
Stamina/perseverance—How I stay with the problem and don't quit			
Focus/time allocation—How I concentrate on the task I am doing and set aside time to practice and understand the concepts in the subject (e.g., geography, culture, groups, institutions, governance)			
Growth mindset—My ability to embrace challenges and mistakes as a path to success			
Social studies strategies—How I use strategies I've acquired in class (e.g., visualizing, drawing, labeling, rereading, highlighting, underlining, giving the final answer)			
Diverse learning styles—How I adapt my learning style to social studies/history, which often requires applying a combination of visual, auditory, and kinesthetic learning styles			
Critical thinking and problem solving—How I adapt to an analytical approach to learning to question assumptions, interpret data, and draw conclusions based on evidence			
Resources—How I use textbooks, manipulatives, online resources, visual aids, anchor charts, or a reflection journal to support my thinking and research			
Seeking help—My ability to self-advocate by asking questions or getting clarification for what I don't understand			

WORKSHEET

Challenges and Strengths Checklist: Science

Quality	This area is a challenge for me.	This area is a strength for me.	This area doesn't apply to me.
Anxiety—How I handle uncomfortable feelings about struggles with science			
Attitude—My confidence, enjoyment, and motivation in science class			
Preparedness—My ability to have all my supplies and everything I need ready for class and to do my homework on time			
Vocabulary load—How I handle science concepts and Tier 3 vocabulary for future use			
Evaluating—My ability to critically examine scientific claims and their support			
Working memory—My ability to hold information in my head while I do another part of the process			
Understanding the task—How I process what's being asked and know what I have to do			
Visual representations—My ability to read and use a large array of visual communication to gain deeper understanding of the text(s) being used			
Thinking like a scientist—How I use cause/effect relationships and connect my everyday experiences to what I am learning in class through reading, discussions, and observations			
Proofreading—My ability to go back over all the steps and check for mistakes			
Stamina/perseverance—How I stay with the problem and don't quit			
Focus/time allocation—How I concentrate on the task I am doing and set aside time to practice and understand the concepts in the subject (e.g., biology, geology, meteorology, chemistry, physics)			
Growth mindset—My ability to embrace challenges and mistakes as a path to success			

Quality	This area is a challenge for me.	This area is a strength for me.	This area doesn't apply to me.
Science strategies—How I use strategies I've acquired in class (e.g., visualizing, drawing, labeling, rereading, highlighting, underlining, giving the final answer)			
Diverse learning styles—How I adapt my learning style to studying science, which often requires applying a combination of visual, auditory, and kinesthetic learning styles			
Critical thinking and problem solving—How I adapt to an analytical approach to learning to question assumptions, interpret data, and draw conclusions based on evidence			
Resources—How I use textbooks, manipulatives, online resources, visual aids, anchor charts, or a reflection journal to support my thinking			
Seeking help—My ability to self-advocate by asking questions or getting clarification for what I don't understand			

WORKSHEET

Challenges and Strengths Checklist: Art

Quality	This area is a challenge for me.	This area is a strength for me.	This area doesn't apply to me.
Anxiety—How I handle uncomfortable feelings about struggles with art			
Attitude—My confidence, enjoyment, and motivation in art class			
Preparedness—My ability to have all my supplies and everything I need ready for class and to do my homework on time			
Vocabulary load—How I handle names of artists, principles of design (e.g., contrast, repetition, harmony, balance), and elements of art (e.g., colors, shapes, textures, forms, values, space, principles, and techniques)			
Interpreting the artist's intentions—My ability to understand the context and perspective of the artwork and the artist			

WORKSHEET

Challenges and Strengths Checklist: Art—(*continued*)

Quality	This area is a challenge for me.	This area is a strength for me.	This area doesn't apply to me.
Self-confidence—My ability to use background knowledge to make sense of the readings, gallery paintings, and/or sculptures, contribute to discussion, and understand the artwork			
Working memory—My ability to hold information in my head along with existing schema to see relevance and importance to our readings, viewings, and classwork			
Understanding the task—How I process what's being asked, know what I have to do, make a plan, and use my understandings to examine and interpret the artwork			
Visual representations—My ability to draw representations and interpret and apply information from a piece of art			
Thinking like an artist—How I use my personal responses to art to evoke emotional responses and connect my own life experiences to what I observe in the artwork			
Proofreading—My ability to revise and edit my responses to short-answer and essay questions			
Stamina/perseverance—How I stay with the problem and don't quit			
Focus—How I concentrate on the task I am doing			
Growth mindset—My ability to embrace challenges and mistakes as a path to success			
Artist strategies—How I use strategies I've learned (e.g., visualizing; drawing; labeling; thinking about what I know about the artist and how they use the principles of design; comparing the artwork with other works of similar time period, theme, method)			
Resources—How I use textbooks, gallery walks, manipulatives, online resources, graphic organizers, personal response, or a reflection journal to support my thinking			
Seeking help—My ability to self-advocate by asking questions or getting clarification for what I don't understand			

Challenges and Strengths Checklist: Health and Physical Education

Quality	This area is a challenge for me.	This area is a strength for me.	This area doesn't apply to me.
Anxiety—How I handle uncomfortable feelings about struggles with health/physical fitness			
Attitude—My confidence, enjoyment, and motivation in health/physical fitness class			
Preparedness—My ability to have all my supplies and everything I need ready for class and to do my homework on time			
Vocabulary load—How I handle health/physical fitness vocabulary and make connections with my own life and the experiences of family and friends			
Application—How my emerging understandings help me change my current behavior and suggest changes to family and friends			
Self-confidence—How I use my background knowledge and experience with sports-related activities and fitness practices to make sense of the readings, contribute to discussion, and understand extracurricular activities offered			
Working memory—My ability to hold information in my head along with existing schema to see relevance and importance to our readings and classwork			
Understanding the task—How I process what's being asked, know what I have to do, and make a plan			
Visual representations—My ability to draw representations and interpret and apply information from a visual (e.g., use a map, draw a graph to represent complex concepts)			
Thinking like a health/physical fitness expert—My understanding of how to stay fit and healthy and explore possibilities for maintaining my physical well-being beyond my school experiences			
Proofreading—My ability to revise and edit my responses to short-answer and essay questions			
Stamina/perseverance—How I stay with the problem and don't quit			

Challenges and Strengths Checklist: Health and Physical Education—(*continued*)

Quality	This area is a challenge for me.	This area is a strength for me.	This area doesn't apply to me.
Focus—How I concentrate on the task I am doing			
Growth mindset—My ability to embrace challenges and mistakes as a path to success			
Health/physical fitness strategies—How I set personal goals with a focus on skill development, involvement, and internalization of the value of being fit and healthy			
Resources—How I use textbooks, manipulatives, online resources, graphic organizers, anchor charts, sports-related activities, or a reflection journal to support my thinking			
Seeking help—My ability to self-advocate by asking questions or getting clarification for what I don't understand			

Appendix L: The Looking Back to Look Ahead Protocol

Look back ... and look ahead.

1. Describe the project you completed or the experiment you conducted.
2. What about the experience surprised you?
3. What about the experience puzzled or frustrated you?
4. When you encountered a problem, how did you solve it?
5. Think about your experience working with classmates on this project/experiment. What went well? What could you have done differently to make your collaboration more efficient or enjoyable?
6. What question(s) about the work or the learning do you have?
7. What was your favorite aspect of the project/experiment? Why?
8. What value could this project/experiment bring to your life?
9. How could reflecting on your learning help you plan a future project on this topic?
10. Will you create another project or conduct a similar experiment? If so, what changes or revisions will you make?

WORKSHEET

Appendix M: The Reflection Roadmap Protocol

You are the explorer! Your thoughts, ideas, sketches, and plans will lead you to the treasure of discovery and success!

The Reflection Roadmap helps you reflect on what you learned, how you learned it, and how you'll plan your final project. Each stop on the map has a question to guide your thinking. It's like a journey through your brain! Follow the arrows from one shape to the next to help you reflect on how you wish your journey to go.

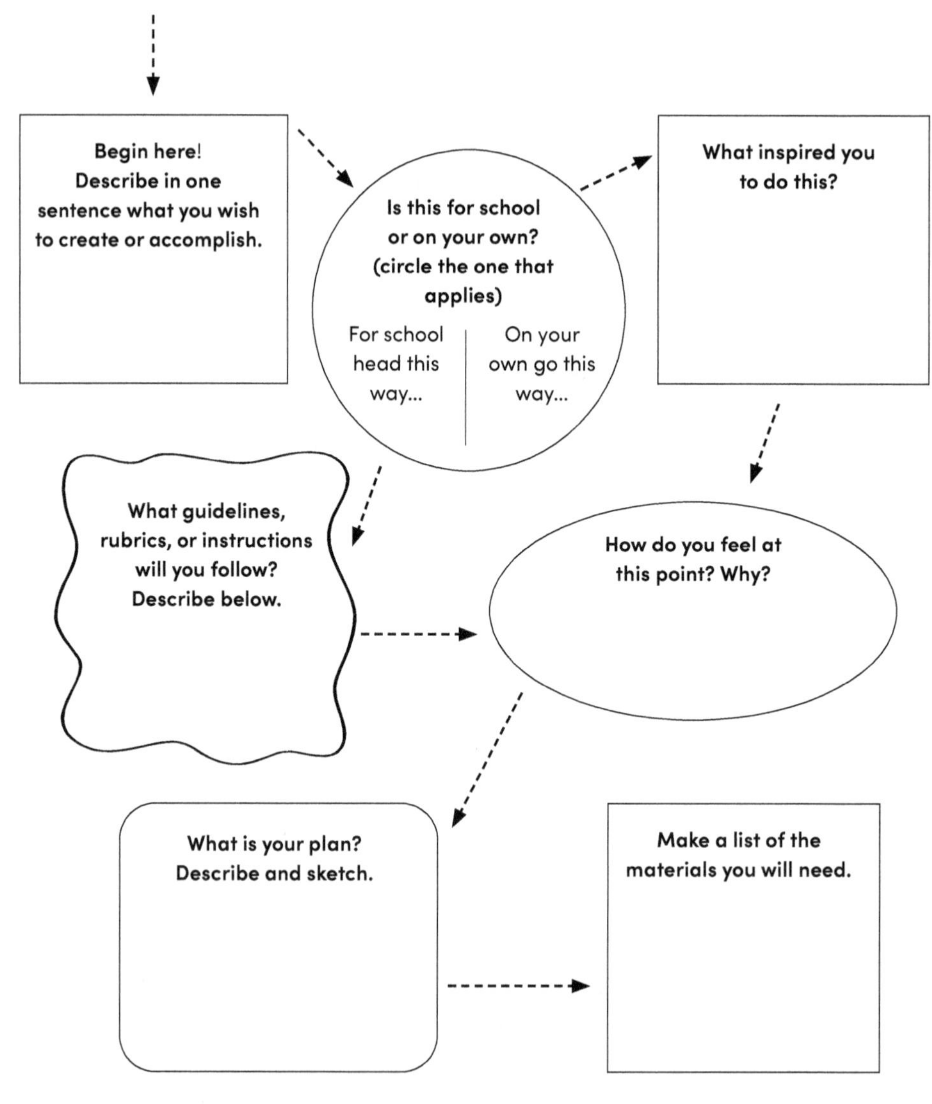

WORKSHEET

Where Do I Go Next?

As with any journey, it's wise to pause along the way to reflect and ask yourself important questions. Here are some to think about:

- **Looking back on learning**
  - What did I discover that can shed light on this project?
  - What was tricky for me when I was learning? How did I work through it?
- **Staying focused**
  - How can I visualize the end product?
  - How will I adapt when something unexpected comes up?
  - What can I do to persevere?
- **Problem solving**
  - What is puzzling me?
  - What caused the problem?
  - How can I retrace my steps?
  - Who can I collaborate with to come up with a solution?
- **Evaluating and reflecting**
  - What worked?
  - What did not work?
  - What surprised me?
  - What would I do differently next time?
  - How did I grow or change as a learner during this time?

A place to reflect and park your thoughts:

WORKSHEET

Appendix N: Two Portfolio Reflection Protocols

Reflection on a Portfolio Artifact

Name: ______________________ Date: ______________

Title of piece: ______________________________

1. I selected this artifact because . . .

2. The strengths of my artifact are . . .

3. If I were going to revise this artifact, I would . . .

because . . . .

WORKSHEET

End-of-Year Reflection on Writing Progress

Respond to the following questions in paragraph form.

1. How has your writer's notebook helped you this year?

2. What revision strategies have worked best for you? Why?

3. What have you learned about yourself as a writer from rereading your notebook?

4. Select two entries from your portfolio that show you understand the qualities of good writing. Explain how these writing pieces demonstrate your understanding.

5. Think about your writing when you first began this grade level (or marking period). How have you changed as a writer?

6. What goals do you still have for your writing? How did you decide on these goals?

Appendix O: The Sticky Note Stretch Protocol

Stretch stems are designed to help you elaborate or expand your thinking. Place a sticky note in the box under each of the four questions. Respond to the question on the sticky note with a word, phrase, or sentence that comes to mind. Then, use one or more **stretch stems** listed to expand on and deepen your original idea in the space to the right. Be specific and give an example for each question. If you run out of room, use the other side of the paper.

WORKSHEET

1. What did you learn about yourself this year, inside and outside the classroom?

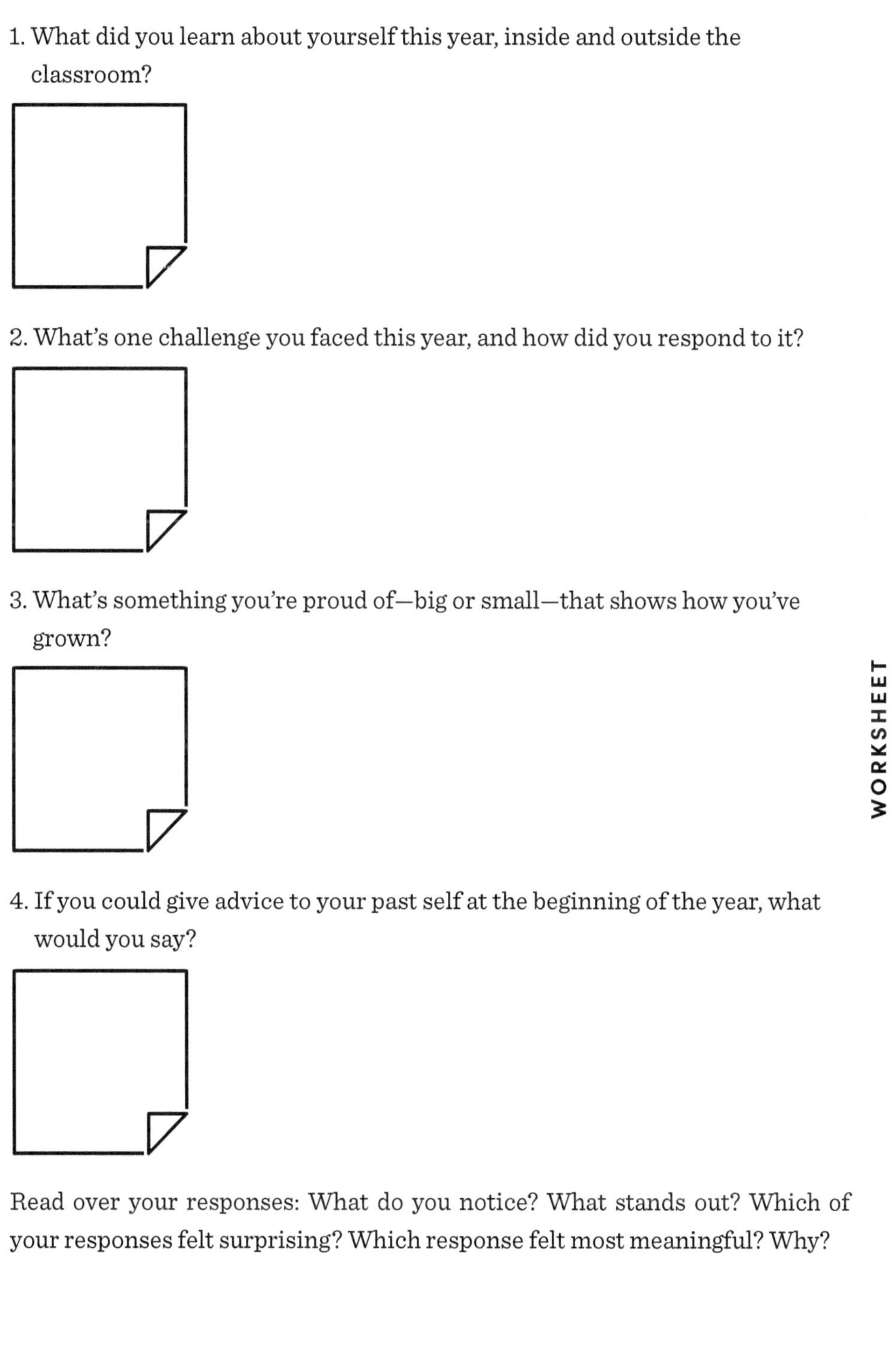

2. What's one challenge you faced this year, and how did you respond to it?

3. What's something you're proud of—big or small—that shows how you've grown?

4. If you could give advice to your past self at the beginning of the year, what would you say?

Read over your responses: What do you notice? What stands out? Which of your responses felt surprising? Which response felt most meaningful? Why?

WORKSHEET

Stretch Stems:

- One specific moment that shaped me was…
- This experience helped me see that I tend to…
- A turning point for me this year was when…
- This stood out to me because…
- Compared to the beginning of the year, now I…
- I could see growth in myself when…
- I learned from this experience that I…
- The mindset that helped me most was…
- The strategy that helped me most was…
- One challenge I faced this year was…
- I struggled with ________, but now…
- I felt ________ when ________ because…
- I'll always remember the moment when ________ because I felt…
- I felt proud when…
- When I faced ________, I felt ________, and that taught me…
- This connects to my life outside school because…
- This connects to my learning in school because…
- I came to understand more of who I am as a learner when…
- If I could go back in time, I would change ________, because…
- This changes the way I think because…
- This experience reminded me that…
- This experience helped me to see that…
- One thing I want to keep doing next year is…
- Next time I face a similar situation, I will choose to…
- One habit I want to strengthen is…
- The pattern I want to break is…
- The way in which I want to grow is…

Appendix P: The Jump-Start Reflection Protocol

Reflection for When You Are Stuck or Stalled

Take a few moments to pause, reflect, and answer the questions below to help jump-start your learning today:

1. Describe what you are learning or what task you are to complete.

2. What are you feeling? Are your feelings a roadblock to moving on?

3. What is preventing you from learning or doing the task?

4. When you've been in a similar situation in the past, what helped jump-start your learning?

5. What adjustments will you make to help you jump-start your learning or task today?

WORKSHEET

WORKSHEET

Stop here and try to engage in your work again. After you finish your learning or task, answer questions 6 to 10.

6. Describe what you learned when you returned to your learning or task.

7. Were you able to complete what you needed to? If so, move on to question 8. If not, talk with your teacher.

8. Reflect on your responses to questions 1 to 5. How did going through and answering those questions help get you jump-started?

9. Write an encouraging message to yourself below.

10. Sketch or write about what you will do next time you struggle to begin.

Appendix Q: A Collection of Nonlinguistic Representation Strategies

To What Extent Do You Agree?

Tape numbers 1 to 5 (1 = "Not at all"; 5 = "I agree completely") in the corners or along one side of your room. Pose a question such as "How well do you understand the big ideas presented in our unit of study?" and have students stand by the number that represents their response.

Thumbs

Have students hold their thumbs up ("You can move on"), sideways ("I sort of get it"), or down ("I don't get it") to show their level of understanding.

Digital Storytelling

Students use images, video, and/or audio to share their thoughts and reflections on their learning.

Fist to Five

To quickly gauge group consensus or individual understanding, have students raise their hands with a number of fingers corresponding to their level of agreement or understanding. A fist (zero fingers) represents strong disagreement or lack of understanding; five fingers represent strong agreement or understanding.

Magnetic Name Cards

Create three columns on the classroom whiteboard labeled "I get it," "I am still wondering/digesting/thinking," and "Not yet." Students post their name cards in the appropriate column to indicate how they feel about their learning in a particular class or subject area.

Strike a Pose

Students strike a pose to express their emotions related to the learning (e.g., powerful, confident, anxious). This technique especially helps kinesthetic learners stay focused and attentive.

Temperature

Students stand in a large circle at the end of a class session or end of day and share a simple statement using one of the prompts below without offering an explanation or trying to defend it.

- I learned that I...
- I relearned that I...
- I realized that I...
- I noticed that I...
- I was confused about...
- I discovered that I...
- I was surprised that I...

Four Corners

Students physically move to different corners of the room, each representing a different perspective or answer choice related to a statement or question. Students can consider viewpoints different from their own, explain their choices, and engage in discussions with their peers.

Collaborative Drawing

Students work together to create a drawing that shows their collective feelings about and understanding of a topic or shared experience.

Appendix R: Reflection Question Sets for Anchor Charts

Reflection as a Magnifying Glass

1. **Foster your observation skills.** *Ask yourself:* What did I focus on today that shows big learning?
2. **Strengthen your self-awareness.** *Ask yourself:* What is something I did on purpose to improve my learning today?
3. **Deepen your understanding.** *Ask yourself:* What did I see that I had not seen before? How does it connect to what I already knew?
4. **Celebrate your growth.** *Ask yourself:* Where did I make progress? How did my thinking shift?
5. **Promote your problem-solving skills.** *Ask yourself:* What is the biggest challenge I faced today? How did I solve it?

Reflection as a Mirror

1. **Increase self-awareness.** *Ask yourself:* What strategies worked best in my learning today? Why? What approach worked best for me in my learning today? Why?
2. **Notice the emotions attached to learning.** *Ask yourself:* How did I feel during my learning today? What might this tell me?
3. **Acknowledge internal changes.** *Ask yourself:* How did my thinking shift during the learning process today? Why is this important?
4. **Explore what you value.** *Ask yourself:* What mattered most to me in my learning today? Why?
5. **Practice honesty.** *Ask yourself:* What is hard for me to admit about myself as a learner today? What is something I can celebrate?

Reflection as a Map

1. **Make a plan.** *Ask yourself:* What is my end goal? What steps do I need to take to get there?
2. **Be aware of the impact of your decisions**. *Ask yourself:* What important decision did I make in my learning today? How did it affect the outcome of my learning?
3. **Practice a growth mindset**. *Ask yourself:* What goal will I set for learning today? What will I need to do to ensure I meet that goal?

4. **Foster a positive learning outlook**. *Ask yourself:* What positive attitudes or mindset can I take with me for future learning?
5. **Connect your learning to real life.** *Ask yourself:* What in my learning can I use in the future?

Appendix S: The Important Thing Protocol, Grades K–3

After reading *The Important Book* by Margaret Wise Brown, have students use the worksheet below to reflect on their learning.

The Important Thing: A Scaffold to Share Your Thinking

1. The most important thing about ________ is...

2. Another interesting fact is...

3. Something that may surprise you is...

4. But the most important thing about ______________ is...

After you've answered the prompts, turn and talk to your partner about your thoughts.

Authors' note: With gratitude to Margaret Wise Brown and *The Important Book*.

WORKSHEET

Appendix T: The Daily Dozen Protocol, Grades 5–12

Select 12 prompts from the list below to post on the board or an anchor chart. Bring closure to the day's learning experiences by asking students to select and respond to two of the listed prompts.

- The thing that made the most sense to me today was...
- One thing that I just don't understand is...
- When someone asks me what I did in ________ class today, I can say...
- One thing I would like more information about is...
- I need more examples of...
- I enjoyed ________ because...
- The most important concept we discussed today was...
- Today's class would have been better if we had...
- One thing I'm still confused about is...
- The hardest thing about today's session was ________ because...
- The thing we did in class today that best fit my learning style was...
- The one thing the teacher did today that best fit my learning style was...
- The one thing the teacher did today that did not work well for me was...
- Here's a point about what we learned today that's crystal clear:...
- One thing that connects with things I already know is...
- Something that connects this class with my world outside the school day is...
- An idea that is still going around in my head is...
- I need to do more reading about...
- I need to do some research on...

Appendix U: The RESET Reflection Wall Protocol

Instructions

Step 1 Prep the chart	1. Divide a large piece of chart paper into five labeled sections: R, E, S, E, T (one for each RESET letter). 2. Assign a sticky note color to each letter (e.g., R = yellow, E = blue).
Step 2 Set up materials	1. Provide each participant with the following: pens, sticky notes in the five colors, and a copy of the RESET reflection questions.
Step 3 Guide the activity	1. Introduce the meaning of each RESET letter and briefly explain the purpose of the reflection. 2. Allow time for participants to reflect and write responses—one or more per letter.
Step 4 Interactive share	1. Invite participants to place their sticky notes in the corresponding section on the chart paper. 2. Facilitate a brief discussion for each letter as notes are added.

RESET Reflection Questions

- **R: Revisit the bright spots**
  - What was the brightest spot of the year?
  - What accomplishments, milestones, or achievements stood out?
  - What unexpected changes or surprises took place?
  - When did you feel most proud?
  - What inspired you?
  - What flourished in your teaching, students, or classroom community?
- **E: Evaluate the challenges, problems, and solutions**
  - What worked? What didn't work?
  - What tested you emotionally or professionally?
  - Where did you struggle or fail? How did you respond?
  - What boundaries or limits were pushed?
  - What obstacles prevented you from moving forward?
- **S: Shifts in perspectives**
  - What changed in the way you think?
  - What changed in how you teach?
  - How did your connections with students and colleagues shift?
  - What was a major revelation for you?
  - What "aha" moment did you experience?
  - When did you show flexibility or adaptability?

- **E: Effort that mattered**
  - Where did your focused energy pay off?
  - What were your most impactful instructional moves?
  - What was an instructional win you'd like to repeat?
  - Where did you persevere and feel proud that you did?
  - What did you do that your students responded to most positively?
- **T: Tomorrow's intentions**
  - What will you carry forward into the next school year?
  - What do you need to let go of or leave behind?
  - What are your hopes and dreams for the year ahead?
  - What goals do you want to set for your next classroom community?
  - What is one key takeaway you want to keep in mind moving forward?
  - How will you rest and restore yourself before the next year begins?

Appendix V: The Reflect, Reframe, Restore Protocol

Teaching is a demanding, fast-paced profession that requires constant juggling of responsibilities. When challenges arise, it can be difficult to slow down and respond in the thoughtful ways we know are best. Reflection can be one of the most valuable and effective ways to shift from an unproductive mindset to one that uncovers possible solutions.

Think about one area of your teaching that has felt especially difficult or frustrating lately. Use the Reflect, Reframe, Restore prompts to record your thinking. While this protocol may not solve everything immediately, it can bring clarity and lead to meaningful steps toward a solution.

REFLECT	Describe in detail an area of your teaching that is especially difficult, challenging, or frustrating. • Name the difficulty, challenge, or problem. • What is the narrative you have been telling yourself? Is it accurate? • What is in your realm of power or control? What is not? • How or where do you feel stuck? • What emotions are involved?
REFRAME	As you think about the difficulty, challenge, or problem, begin to imagine it through a different, more constructive lens. • *I wonder if the problem is really about . . .* • *If I were to stand in someone else's shoes, I would . . .* • *What would happen if I modified . . . ?* • *A pattern that has emerged is . . .* • *One thing I'm doing well, despite the challenge, is . . .* • *A resource or trusted colleague who could help me with this is . . .* • *I realize now that . . .*
RESTORE	When teaching gets hard, it's easy to feel stuck in what feels broken, lost, or unclear. Describe how you can rebuild what is broken, re-establish what is lost, and redefine what is unclear. Ground yourself in a new possibility. • *A boundary to establish is . . .* • *I know now that . . .* • *Hopes and dreams I have for this are . . .* • *I believe the solution lies in . . .* • *It's possible that . . .*

References

Afflerbach, P., Cho, B.-Y., Kim, J.-Y., Crassas, M. E., & Doyle, B. (2013). Reading: What else matters besides strategies and skills? *The Reading Teacher, 66*(6), 440–448. https://doi.org/10.1002/TRTR.1146

Alberini, C. M., & Kandel, E. R. (2014). The regulation of transcription in memory consolidation. *Cold Spring Harbor Perspectives in Biology, 7,* a021741. https://doi.org/10.1101/cshperspect.a021741

Atwell, N. (1998). *In the middle: New understandings about writing, reading, and learning* (2nd ed.). Boynton/Cook.

Bain, J. D., Ballantyne, R., Mills, C., & Lester, N. C. (2002). *Reflecting on practice: Student teachers' perspectives.* Post Pressed.

Black, P., & Wiliam, D. (2010). Inside the black box: Raising standards through classroom assessment. *Phi Delta Kappan, 92*(1), 81–90. https://doi.org/10.1177/003172171009200119

Borton, T. (1970). *Reach, touch, and teach: Student concerns and process education.* McGraw-Hill.

Boud, D., Keogh, R., & Walker, D. (Eds.). (1985). *Reflection: Turning experience into learning.* Routledge.

Boyd, L. (2015, December 15). *After watching this, your brain will not be the same* [Video]. YouTube. https://youtu.be/LNHBMFCzznE

Britton, J. N. (1970). *Language and learning.* University of Miami Press.

Brown, M. W. (1999). *The important book.* HarperCollins.

Carey, B. (2015). *How we learn: The surprising truth about when, where, and why it happens.* Random House Trade.

Clear, J. (2018). *Atomic habits: An easy & proven way to build good habits & break bad ones.* Avery.

Dawson, P., & Guare, R. (2009). *Smart but scattered: The revolutionary "executive skills" approach to helping kids reach their potential.* Guilford.

de la Peña, M. (2015). *Last stop on Market Street.* G. P. Putnam's Sons.

Dewey, J. (1933). *How we think: A restatement of the relation of reflective thinking to the educative process.* D. C. Heath.

Di Stefano, G., Gino, F., Pisano, G., & Staats, B. (2023). *Learning by thinking: How reflection can spur progress along the learning curve.* (Harvard Business School NOM Unit Working Paper No. 14-093; Kenan Institute of Private Enterprise Research Paper No. 2414478). https://doi.org/10.2139/ssrn.2414478

Donohoo, J., Hattie, J., & Eells, R. (2018). *The power of collective efficacy.* Corwin.

Dorfman, L., & Capelli, R. (2017). *Mentor texts: Teaching writing through children's literature, K–6* (2nd ed.). Routledge.

Dweck, C. S. (2006). *Mindset: The new psychology of success.* Random House.

Ellis, S., Carette, B., Anseel, F., & Lievens, F. (2014). Systematic reflection: Implications for learning from failures and successes. *Current Directions in Psychological Science, 23*(1), 67–72. https://doi.org/10.1177/0963721413504106

Emerson, R. W. (1996). *Hitch your wagon to a star and other quotations from Ralph Waldo Emerson* (K. Frome, Ed.). Columbia University Press.

Fullan, M. (1993a). *Change forces: Probing the depth of educational reform.* Falmer.

Fullan, M. (1993b). Why teachers must become change agents. *Educational Leadership, 50*(6), 12–16. https://www.ascd.org/el/articles/why-teachers-must-become-change-agents

Gallagher, K. (2011). *Write like this: Teaching real-world writing through modeling & mentor texts.* Stenhouse.

Hagan, C., Callison, M., & Fox, A. (2020). The RECAP and SCAFFOLDS frameworks: Engaging students in self-reflection and self-regulation within online learning. *Journal of Teaching and Learning with Technology, 9*(1), 36–63. https://doi.org/10.14434/jotlt.v9i1.29469

Hallstead, T., & Nash, E. (2020). Meta-talks: How a supplemental instructor fosters student reflection through everyday data. *The Learning Assistance Review, 25*(1), 103–128. https://files.eric.ed.gov/fulltext/EJ1252329.pdf

Hattie, J. (2009). *Visible learning: A synthesis of over 800 meta-analyses relating to achievement.* Routledge.

Himmele, P., & Himmele, W. (2017). *Total participation techniques: Making every student an active learner* (2nd ed.). ASCD.

Holmes, O. W. (2006). *The autocrat of the breakfast table.* Echo Library. Original work published 1858.

Hughes, S., Lyddy, F., & Lambe, S. (2013). Misconceptions about psychological science: A review. *Psychology Learning & Teaching, 12*(1), 20–31. https://doi.org/10.2304/plat.2013.12.1.20

Iordanou, K. (2022). Supporting strategic and meta-strategic development of argument skill: The role of reflection. *Metacognition and Learning, 17,* 399–425. https://doi.org/10.1007/s11409-021-09289-1

Iordanou, K., & Rapanta, C. (2021). "Argue with me": A method for developing argument skills. *Frontiers in Psychology, 12,* 631203. https://doi.org/10.3389/fpsyg.2021.631203

Kierkegaard, S. (2008). *Kierkegaard's journals and notebooks: Volume 2, Journals EE–KK* (N. J. Cappelørn, A. Hannay, D. Kangas, B. H. Kirmmse, V. Rumble & K. B. Söderquist, Eds.). Princeton University Press.

King, H., & Tran, L. (2017). Facilitating deep conceptual learning: The role of reflection and learning communities. In P. G. Patrick (Ed.), *Preparing informal science educators: Perspectives from science communication and education* (pp. 67–85). Springer.

Kramer Ertel, P. A. (2021). Key principles and strategies for enhancing student engagement and learning. *Kappa Delta Pi Record, 57*(3), 120–125. https://doi.org/10.1080/00228958.2021.1935504

Kuhn, D., Hemberger, L., & Khait, V. (2016). *Argue with me: Argument as a path to developing students' thinking and writing* (2nd ed.). Routledge.

Larrivee, B. (2000). Transforming teaching practice: Becoming the critically reflective teacher. *Reflective Practice, 1*(3), 293–307. https://doi.org/10.1080/713693162

Lew, M. D. N., & Schmidt, H. G. (2011). Self-reflection and academic performance: Is there a relationship? *Advances in Health Sciences Education, 16,* 529–545. https://doi.org/10.1007/s10459-011-9298-z

Popham, W. J. (2018). *Classroom assessment: What teachers need to know* (8th ed.). Pearson Education.

Porter, J. (Winter, 2019). Why you should make time for self-reflection (even if you hate doing it). *Harvard Business Review,* 39–40.

Right Question Institute. (n.d.). *What is the QFT?* https://rightquestion.org/what-is-the-qft/

Ritchhart, R., Turner, T., & Hadar, L. (2009). Uncovering students' thinking about thinking using concept maps. *Metacognition and Learning, 4,* 145–159. https://doi.org/10.1007/s11409-009-9040-x

Rothstein, D., & Santana, L. (2011). *Make just one change: Teach students to ask their own questions.* Harvard Education Press.

Routman, R. (2003). *Reading essentials: The specifics you need to teach reading well.* Heinemann.

Routman, R. (2018). *Literacy essentials: Engagement, excellence, and equity for all learners* (2nd ed.). Stenhouse.

Sajna Jaleel, P. P. (2016). A study on the metacognitive awareness of secondary school students. *Universal Journal of Educational Research, 4*(1), 165–172. https://doi.org/10.13189/ujer.2016.040121

Schön, D. A. (1983). *The reflective practitioner: How professionals think in action.* Basic Books.

Siegel, D. J., & Bryson, T. P. (2012). *The whole-brain child: 12 revolutionary strategies to nurture your child's developing mind.* Bantam.

Siegel, D. J., & Drulis, C. (2023). An interpersonal neurobiology perspective on the mind and mental health: Personal, public, and planetary well-being. *Annals of General Psychiatry, 22,* Article 5. https://doi.org/10.1186/s12991-023-00434-5

Sousa, D. A. (2023). *Engaging the rewired brain.* Corwin Press.

Tamimi, M. A. M. A. (2024). Effects of digital story-telling on motivation, critical thinking, and academic achievement in secondary school English learners. *Research in Social Sciences and Technology, 9*(1), 305–328. https://doi.org/10.46303/ressat.2024.18

Tanner, K. D. (2012). Promoting student metacognition. *CBE—Life Sciences Education, 11*(2), 113–120. https://doi.org/10.1187/cbe.12-03-0033

Taylor, K., & Rohrer, D. (2010). The effects of interleaved practice. *Applied Cognitive Psychology, 24*(1), 837–848. https://doi.org/10.1002/acp.1598

Tovani, C. (2011). *So what do they really know? Assessment that informs teaching and learning.* Stenhouse.

Willis, J., & Willis, M. (2020). *Research-based strategies to ignite student learning: Insights from neuroscience and the classroom.* ASCD.

Wolf, K., & Siu-Runyan, Y. (1996). Portfolio purposes and possibilities. *Journal of Adolescent & Adult Literacy, 40*(1), 30–37. http://www.jstor.org/stable/40012110

Yale University Poorvu Center for Teaching and Learning. (n.d.). *Learning styles as a myth.* https://poorvucenter.yale.edu/teaching/teaching-resource-library/learning-styles-as-a-myth

Yeager, D. S., & Dweck, C. S. (2012). Mindsets that promote resilience: When students believe that personal characteristics can be developed. *Educational Psychologist, 47*(4), 302–314. https://doi.org/10.1080/00461520.2012.722805

Zeichner, K. M., & Liston, D. P. (1996). *Reflective teaching: An introduction.* L. Erlbaum Associates.

Zimmerman, B. J. (2002). Becoming a self-regulated learner: An overview. *Theory into Practice, 41*(2), 64–70. https://doi.org/10.1207/s15430421tip4102_2

Zinsser, W. (1993). *Writing to learn.* HarperPerennial.

Zohar, A., & Peled, B. (2008). The effects of explicit teaching of metastrategic knowledge on low- and high-achieving students. *Learning and Instruction, 18*(4), 337–353. https://doi.org/10.1016/j.learninstruc.2007.07.001

Index

The letter *f* following a page locator denotes a figure. The letters *qr* following a page locater denote a QR code.

About the Authors

Lynne Dorfman, EdD, has 38 years of experience in Upper Moreland Township School District as a classroom teacher, gifted education teacher K–5, writing coach, literacy coach, reading specialist, and staff developer. She's an adjunct professor for Arcadia University, an independent literacy consultant, and an advisory board member for West Chester Writing Project. Lynne enjoys her work as a co-editor of *PA Reads: Journal of Keystone State Literacy Association* and as Pennsylvania Alpha Delta Kappa President (2026–2028). Dr. Dorfman is the coauthor of nine books, including *Mentor Texts: Teaching Writing Through Children's Literature, K–6; Welcome to Writing Workshop*; and *Welcome to Reading Workshop*. Lynne has presented at many conferences, including ILA, PCTELA, NCTE, RCCNA, KSLA, CCIRA, Missouri Write to Learn, Alabama State Literacy Association, and Literacy for All.

Catherine Gehman, MEd, has devoted more than 25 years to classroom teaching, work she considers the most meaningful part of her career. A National Writing Project fellow, she brings the project's emphasis on writer identity, reflection, and authentic voice into her 4th grade English language arts classroom in Pennsylvania. Catherine has served primary, intermediate, and middle grade students in New York, Iowa, and Pennsylvania, including English learners and students with disabilities. She is passionate about cultivating communities where all learners feel safe, valued, and connected. Beyond her classroom, she leads professional development in her district and presents locally and at state and national levels, including KSLA, PCTELA, and NCTE, sharing practical, research-informed, ready-to-use strategies that help students understand their thinking, reflect with intention, and grow as learners.

Pérsida Himmele, PhD, is a professor of teacher education at Millersville University in Pennsylvania, where she has taught for more than 20 years. She has 10 years of public school experience as an elementary and middle school bilingual and multilingual classroom teacher in New York and California and as a district administrator in Pennsylvania. She has been a consultant to various school districts, the Pennsylvania Department of Education, and educational entities around the world. Pérsida and her husband, William, are the authors of several ASCD books and resources, including the bestseller *Total Participation Techniques: Making Every Student an Active Learner*. She can be reached via her website at totalparticipationtechniques.com.

Aileen Hower, EdD, is an associate professor of literacy education at Millersville University in Pennsylvania, where she serves as the coordinator for the Language and Literacy Masters graduate program and teaches graduate and undergraduate courses. She has 16 years of Pennsylvania teaching and administrative experience as a reading specialist and high school English teacher, and an additional six years as a PK–12 literacy supervisor. Aileen is passionately involved with many state and national literacy organizations, such as the International Literacy Association and the Keystone State Literacy Association, where she has served as president and ILA coordinator. She is also on the board of trustees at The Janus School, a school for students who learn differently. Aileen is the coauthor of *Centering ELLs in the Science of Reading* (Quick Reference Guide) with ASCD and has written various articles focusing on language and literacy. She can be reached via her faculty page on the Millersville University website.

About ISTE+ASCD

ISTE+ASCD's mission is to empower educators to reimagine and redesign learning through impactful pedagogy and meaningful technology use. We achieve this by offering transformative professional learning, cultivating and disseminating thought leadership, fostering vibrant communities, and ensuring that digital tools and experiences are accessible and effective.

Related Books and Resources

At the time of publication, the following resources related to this book's topic were available:

Building Teacher Capacity Through Reflection by Pete Hall and Alisa A. Simeral (Quick Reference Guide)

Developing Growth Mindsets: Principles and Practices for Maximizing Student Potential by Donna Wilson and Marcus Conyers (Book)

Learning and Leading with Habits of Mind: 16 Essential Characteristics for Success by Arthur L. Costa and Bena Kallick (Book)

Learning by Mistake: 12 Strategies to Turn Student Errors into Opportunities by Emma Chiappetta (Book)

Questioning for Formative Feedback: Meaningful Dialogue to Improve Learning by Jackie Acree Walsh (Book)

Social-Emotional Learning and the Brain: Strategies to Help Your Students Thrive by Marilee Sprenger (Book)

Stretch Yourself: A Personalized Journey to Deepen Your Teaching Practice by Caitlin McLemore & Fanny Passeport (Book)

Student-Led Assessment: Promoting Agency and Achievement Through Portfolios and Conferences by Starr Sackstein (Book)

Teaching for Deeper Learning: Tools to Engage Students in Meaning Making by Jay McTighe and Harvey F. Silver (Book)

Teaching Students to Drive Their Brains: Metacognitive Strategies, Activities, and Lessons by Donna Wilson and Marcus Conyers (Book)

For up-to-date information about ISTE+ASCD resources, go to iste-ascd.org/books. To learn more about membership and join or renew, go to iste-ascd.org/membership, email memsupport@iste-ascd.org, or call 1-800-933-2723 or 703-578-9600.

www.ingramcontent.com/pod-product-compliance
Lightning Source LLC
LaVergne TN
LVHW080847170826
845678LV00006B/1737